THE PINK SALT TRICK RECIPE FOR WEIGHT LOSS

THE NATURAL 21-DAY RITUAL TO BURN FAT, BEAT BLOATING, AND FEEL ENERGIZED WITHOUT COUNTING CALORIES OR GIVING UP THE FOODS YOU LOVE

JENNIFER A. FALKNER

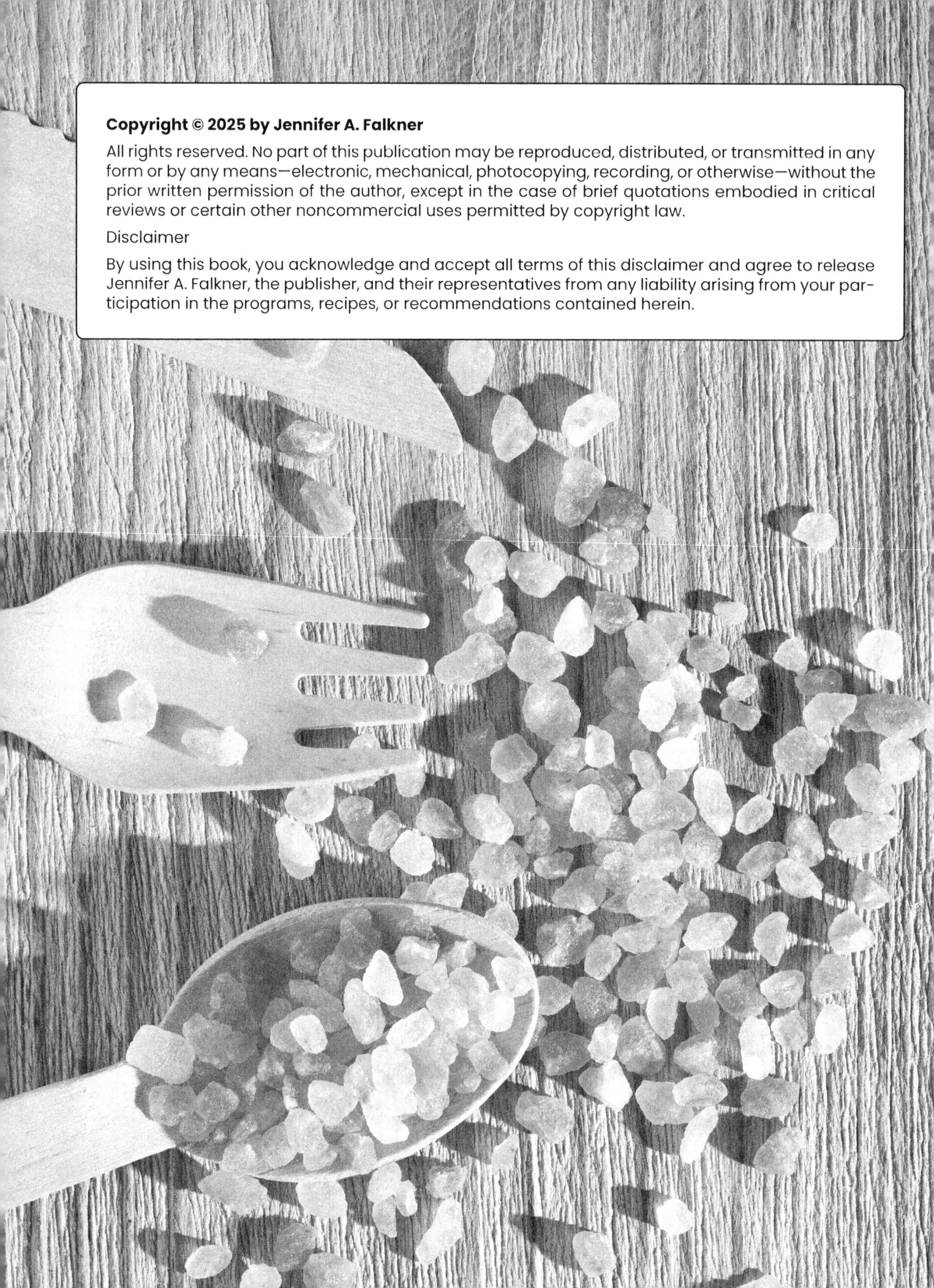

Copyright © 2025 by Jennifer A. Falkner

All rights reserved. No part of this publication may be reproduced, distributed, or transmitted in any form or by any means—electronic, mechanical, photocopying, recording, or otherwise—without the prior written permission of the author, except in the case of brief quotations embodied in critical reviews or certain other noncommercial uses permitted by copyright law.

Disclaimer

By using this book, you acknowledge and accept all terms of this disclaimer and agree to release Jennifer A. Falkner, the publisher, and their representatives from any liability arising from your participation in the programs, recipes, or recommendations contained herein.

TABLE OF CONTENTS

INTRODUCTION 6
Why the Pink Salt Trick Isn't Just a Trend 6
What You Can Expect from This Book 7
How to Use This Guide for Real Results 9

CHAPTER 1
WHAT IS THE PINK SALT TRICK? 12
The Origins: From Ayurveda to TikTok 12
Why It Works: Hydration, Minerals, and Hormonal Balance 14
What Makes It Different From Other "Detox" Trends 16

CHAPTER 2
THE CORE RECIPE 19
The Pink Salt Morning Elixir: Ingredients & Step-by-Step Prep 19
FAQs: When to Drink It, On an Empty Stomach, Safety, and More 21
Optional Add-Ins: Lemon, Ginger, Apple Cider Vinegar, Honey 23

CHAPTER 3
THE SCIENCE BEHIND THE SIP 26
How Pink Salt Affects Digestion, Bloating, and Cravings 26
Real Nutrient Functions (Explained Simply) 28
The Truth About Salt and Weight Loss 30

CHAPTER 4
THE 21-DAY PINK SALT RITUAL PLAN 33
How to Build a Daily Wellness Habit 33
Week-by-Week Focus (Hydration → Digestion → Energy Boost) 35
Troubleshooting Common Issues (Cravings, Headaches, Fatigue) 36

CHAPTER 5
THE PINK SALT-FRIENDLY MEAL BLUEPRINT 39
Foods That Complement the Trick (Anti-Inflammatory & Light) 39
What to Avoid (Without Restrictive Dieting) 40
Sample Daily Eating Rhythm (No Counting, No Tracking) 42

CHAPTER 6
DRINK & SNACK RECIPES FOR WELLNESS SUPPORT 45
Detox Waters with Pink Salt 45
Natural Electrolyte Blends for Energy 47
Gut-Loving Smoothies & Satisfying Sips 49

CHAPTER 7
THE 5-MINUTE MORNING RITUAL THAT CHANGES EVERYTHING 52
Drink with Intention 52
Gratitude First, Goals Second 54
Gentle Movement (Optional but Powerful) 56
Tune In, Not Scroll Down 57
Keep It Light, But Consistent 59

CHAPTER 8
TROUBLESHOOTING & REAL-LIFE ADAPTATION 62
What If You Miss a Day? 62
Dealing with Cravings and PMS 64
How to Travel with the Trick 66
Adjusting for Cold Weather, Work Life, or Family Routine 68

CHAPTER 9
SMART TOOLS TO SUPPORT YOUR ROUTINE 70
Pink Salt Ritual Prep Checklist 70
"Swap This for That" Clean Salt Chart 72
"Salt + Glow" Self-Care Weekly Guide 74

CHAPTER 10
GOING BEYOND WEIGHT LOSS 77
How to Shift from Quick Fixes to Long-Term Glow 77
Building a Wellness Identity, Not Just a Goal 79
Final Words: You Are Not Starting Over—You're Evolving 80

APPENDICES
BONUS SECTION 83
Quick FAQ Recap: Your top questions, clearly answered 83
Morning Ritual Journal Pages (Guided): For personal reflection and mindset anchoring 85
7-Day Reset Reflection Sheet 88

Introduction

WHY THE PINK SALT TRICK ISN'T JUST A TREND

Every few months, there's a new health "trick" lighting up your social media feed. Celery juice. Chlorophyll drops. Lemon coffee. Most of them vanish as fast as they appear—replaced by the next big promise in a bottle, a blender, or a capsule. So why is the pink salt trick different? Why is it still being talked about, reshared, and recommended long after the first viral video faded?

To answer that, you have to understand what it taps into: not just a desire to lose weight, but something deeper. It connects with a growing movement—especially among women—toward simple, natural practices that actually feel good to do. It's a response to years of being bombarded by extreme diets, synthetic supplements, and plans that require more discipline than most busy people can realistically give. The pink salt trick isn't trying to change your entire life in a week. It's designed to *fit into* your life—your mornings, your metabolism, your need for something that actually helps you feel better, fast.

From TikTok to Ayurveda: The Layers Behind the Trend

If you've ever sipped warm water with a pinch of pink Himalayan salt, maybe with a squeeze of lemon, you already know the basics. It's simple. But what's often missed is how far this "trick" actually reaches—both forward in terms of current wellness culture, and backward into ancient wisdom.

This ritual didn't start on TikTok. The roots stretch back to Ayurvedic traditions, where warm saltwater was used to stimulate digestion and bring balance to the body. In Traditional Chinese Medicine, mineral salts were used to support kidney function and hydration. These systems weren't based on calories or macros—they were based on listening to the body, on rhythms, on nature.

What modern wellness has done is repackage that wisdom in a way that resonates with women today. The pink salt trick feels like something your grandmother might have sworn by, but also like something your favorite influencer might demo during a "5-minute morning reset." That's the sweet spot. It's old and new at the same time.

Why It Keeps Spreading

People don't keep doing something that doesn't work. The reason this ritual keeps showing up in wellness spaces is because—for many—it delivers something noticeable, quickly. Bloating goes down. Energy goes up. That groggy, sluggish morning fog? Gone before the coffee even kicks in.

This isn't a placebo effect. It's basic physiology. When you wake up, your body is slightly dehydrated. Your stress hormones are already rising. Your stomach acid is either too low or out of balance. The right combination of mineral-rich salt, water, and optional acid (like lemon or apple cider vinegar) helps support your adrenal function, digestion, and cellular hydration. These aren't vague wellness buzzwords. They're chemical processes your body goes through every single morning. The salt trick simply supports those processes in a natural, non-invasive way.

There's also a psychological layer. When a woman begins her day with *something she's doing for herself*, that morning ritual becomes more than a drink. It's a mental reset. A moment of control. It says, "Before I respond to everyone else's needs today, I'm going to respond to mine." That's powerful. And it's part of what keeps this ritual from fading into the background with the rest of the wellness noise.

It's Simple, But Not Simplistic

Some people dismiss it because it's too easy. How could something so basic have real value? But ask any woman who's tried complicated systems, expensive powders, or 45-minute fasting protocols—they'll tell you: simple is the only thing that sticks.

And not all simplicity is created equal. The pink salt trick works not because it's trendy, but because it touches on a *need*. We live in a culture of overconsumption—over-stimulation, over-planning, over-thinking every bite of food. This ritual is a way to strip that back. To hydrate, balance, and soothe your system with something that feels intuitive.

It doesn't demand a new identity. You don't need to buy a \$300 juicer or change your entire diet. It meets you where you are, with ingredients you probably already have in your kitchen.

Why It Resonates With Women—Especially Now

Something shifted during the past few years. Between the pandemic, rising stress levels, and increased awareness of burnout and hormone disruption, women are no longer chasing "skinny" at all costs. They're chasing energy. Confidence. That light, clean, sharp feeling of waking up not just lighter, but more clear-headed, less inflamed.

The pink salt trick is part of a larger response to that shift. It doesn't promise a bikini body in ten days. What it offers is a consistent, nourishing ritual that makes women feel more connected to their bodies—and more likely to trust those bodies again.

That trust has been eroded by years of crash diets, restrictive eating, and products that worked for a week and then backfired. The pink salt ritual doesn't punish or restrict. It supports. And support is the keyword here—it's the emotional backbone of this method.

It's Also Evolving

The trick itself has grown. Some women add ginger for digestion. Others add lemon for alkalinity. Some include a spoon of honey or a splash of apple cider vinegar. It's customizable, flexible, and open-ended—exactly how modern routines need to be. No rules, just suggestions. That's another reason it hasn't burned out like so many other trends: it evolves with you.

It also adapts across seasons. Warm in winter, cold in summer. Paired with gentle movement or simply sipped while journaling. It bends without breaking, and that's rare in wellness protocols.

So while the pink salt trick might *look* like just another health fad, the reality is more grounded. It taps into real human physiology. It honors traditional wisdom. It empowers women to take action without restriction or shame. And perhaps most importantly—it makes sense in a real life, with real responsibilities, on real mornings.

WHAT YOU CAN EXPECT FROM THIS BOOK

If you're holding this book in your hands—or scrolling through it on your device—it's probably because you're looking for something that fits into your life without flipping it upside down. Maybe you've tried other wellness methods that were too rigid, too complicated, or just too unrealistic.

Maybe you're tired of promising yourself you'll start fresh on Monday, only to feel discouraged by Wednesday. You're not alone, and this book isn't going to add to that noise.

What you'll find here is not just a pink salt drink recipe. It's a system—a framework—for introducing gentle wellness into your routine in a way that actually sticks. This isn't about quick fixes or gimmicks. It's about building small, reliable habits that support how you want to feel: lighter, clearer, more energized, and more in tune with your body.

A Clear Structure That Honors Your Time

Let's start with what you'll get, practically speaking. This book is laid out in a way that makes it easy to jump in—no background in wellness required. Whether you're completely new to the pink salt ritual or already dabbling in "that girl" TikTok routines, the content is layered to meet you where you are.

You'll get:

- A clear explanation of what the pink salt trick actually is, where it came from, and why it works physiologically—not just trendy claims but real mechanisms in the body that make it useful.
- A step-by-step breakdown of how to prepare and use the pink salt elixir, including variations to suit your taste and needs.
- An accessible look at the science behind how this drink supports digestion, energy, hydration, and metabolism, explained in plain language.
- A 21-day ritual plan to help you turn this from a one-off experiment into a morning habit you look forward to.
- Tips on food pairing, meal rhythm, and lifestyle tweaks that can gently amplify your results—without needing to overhaul your entire diet.
- Simple recipes for wellness-supporting drinks and snacks that fit into real schedules, including morning smoothies and natural electrolyte blends.
- A framework for building a five-minute morning ritual that centers your body and mind—because the pink salt trick works even better when paired with intention and mindfulness.
- Guides and tools to help you stay on track, including checklists, mini trackers, and customizable ritual pages.
- Real-life adaptations for those "off" days—because life happens, and wellness should bend, not break.

This isn't a book that assumes you live in a vacuum. It's been written with full-time jobs, families, stress, and bad sleep in mind. It's designed to work whether your mornings are chaotic or quiet. If you're consistent, even just loosely, you'll start to notice real changes. And not just on the scale—though that may happen too. More energy. Less bloating. Sharper focus. Clearer skin. And, perhaps most important, more confidence in your ability to take care of yourself without guilt or drama.

A Voice That Speaks to Your Real Life

You won't find judgment here. This book doesn't wag its finger at you for not drinking a green smoothie every day or skipping a workout. It doesn't assume you're living on endless free time or disposable income. Instead, it talks to you like a friend who's been through the chaos and found something that works—not because it's perfect, but because it's doable.

You'll notice the tone is straightforward, warm, and curious. It's written with empathy, not hype. It's backed by information that's been simplified, not dumbed down. You'll feel guided, not lectured. You'll see nuance—because no two bodies are the same, and what works beautifully for one person might need a tweak for someone else.

That nuance matters. For example, if you have low blood pressure, or if you're pregnant or breastfeeding, the way you approach this ritual may need to be adjusted. This book gives you the knowledge and options to make informed choices. It doesn't pretend to replace your doctor. It gives you something more subtle—awareness, habit, and agency.

You'll Be Supported with Tools, Not Tasks

One of the biggest reasons people stop trying to take care of themselves is that wellness starts to feel like another full-time job. Another thing to fail at. That's not what you need. What you need is a simple tool you can actually use every day—without it turning into homework.

So, you'll get light, supportive extras along the way. Small daily wins. Tiny shifts in mindset. Templates you can use if you like planning, or skip entirely if you don't. Flexibility is built into this process.

You won't be expected to follow a rigid 45-minute protocol. You'll be invited to choose what feels right, from sipping the elixir while your kids are still asleep, to doing a short stretch while it settles in your stomach. The point is to create space in your day that's just for you. And once you realize how good that feels, it becomes something you want to do—not something you have to do.

What You Won't Find Here

Let's also be clear about what this book isn't. It's not going to give you fake before-and-after photos, celebrity endorsements, or promises of losing ten pounds in three days. It's not packed with filler content or generic wellness advice you could Google in five minutes.

Instead, it offers thoughtful, well-researched content grounded in actual results—both from user experience and scientific data. Where the science is strong, it's explained clearly. Where the science is still developing, it's acknowledged honestly.

This book isn't a sales pitch. It's a toolset. It's here to give you something to reach for on the mornings when you need support, and to teach you how to listen to your body on the days it asks for something different. It respects your time, your intelligence, and your real life.

A Book That Lives on Your Counter, Not Your Shelf

If this works the way it's meant to, you won't finish the book and file it away. You'll leave it on the kitchen counter or bedside table. You'll flip through the meal rhythms, re-read the morning ritual section when your schedule gets hectic, and maybe scribble notes in the journaling pages.

It's meant to grow with you—not to dictate who you should be. Because the truth is, you're already enough. This book just gives you one more way to take care of that "enough" with a little more grace, a little more presence, and a little more ease.

HOW TO USE THIS GUIDE FOR REAL RESULTS

Before we get into routines, recipes, and ritual plans, let's be honest about something: having good information doesn't always translate into actual change. If it did, half the people with wellness books on their shelves would already be feeling amazing every day. The real challenge isn't learning something new—it's figuring out how to use it *consistently* in real life. That's what this guide was built for.

This isn't a book you read once and file away. It's designed to live with you—on your counter, in your bag, bookmarked and a little worn. Every section is written to be used, not just read. You don't need to follow everything perfectly. In fact, if you do this book "imperfectly" but consistently, you'll likely still notice meaningful results. The key is to approach this with the mindset of building a flexible habit, not chasing a perfect outcome.

Read It Like a Recipe, Not a Rulebook

If you've ever cooked from instinct rather than a strict formula, you already know how this works. The pink salt ritual isn't rigid. It has guidelines, yes—but it's not all or nothing. You'll get the basic recipe, the optional add-ins, and the timing suggestions, but what you do with that information is up to you. If you're someone who loves structure, you can follow the 21-day plan, check off each box, and track how you feel. If structure stresses you out, just make the drink each morning and let that be enough.

The important thing is to actually try it. Not for one morning. For at least a week—ideally three. This guide gives you everything you need to make that feel manageable. You'll find tips for busy mornings, suggestions for adjusting based on season or mood, and even ways to use the ritual while traveling. You won't have to figure it out alone.

Go Beyond the Drink: Use the Tools

The elixir is the anchor of this system, but the book offers more than just what to put in your glass. Each chapter was created to support a part of your routine that might be dragging you down—whether it's your eating rhythm, energy levels, digestion, or mindset.

You'll see specific tools, like:

- Mini checklists to help you prep your morning in under five minutes.
- Guided journal pages for setting intentions and noticing patterns in how you feel.
- A weekly self-care planner that connects the pink salt habit to broader wellness goals.
- Meal pairing suggestions to keep your system light and steady, not spiking and crashing.
- Simple recipes that take 10 minutes or less and support gut health and hydration.

These aren't there to impress—they're there to be used. Write in the margins. Highlight the parts that click. Skip what doesn't. You're not being graded. You're building awareness, and awareness is what creates change that lasts.

Adapt the Framework to Your Life

You don't have to change who you are to get results from this guide. You don't need a meditation room or a fancy blender. Whether you're a stay-at-home mom navigating school drop-offs or a full-time worker powering through morning meetings, the framework bends around you.

Maybe you like to start your day before everyone else in the house is up. Great—make your salt drink, sit for a few quiet moments, and take a breath. Maybe your mornings are chaotic, and the best you can do is mix it in a travel cup and sip it during your commute. That works too. The book will show you how to make this process suit your pace.

You'll also find options for how to handle "off" days. Days when you forget. Days when you oversleep. Days when you're traveling or feeling under the weather. The ritual doesn't fall apart if you skip it—it simply pauses. And this guide includes suggestions for how to jump back in without guilt or overthinking.

Use Reflection to Keep It Real

If you're like most readers of this book, you've probably tried other wellness plans before. Maybe they started strong, and then life got in the way. One reason that happens is because we don't stop to check in. We treat wellness like a finish line rather than something alive and responsive.

That's why this guide invites you to reflect—not obsess, just notice. There are prompts throughout that ask questions like:

- How did I feel waking up today?
- What felt light in my body after the elixir—and what didn't?
- When did I feel most in sync with myself this week?

You don't have to answer these in a journal if that's not your style. You can just keep them in your head as you move through your day. But the more you reflect, the more data you gather about *you*. And that's what helps the habit stick—not motivation, but personal feedback.

Track Progress Without Obsessing

Tracking doesn't mean measuring your waist or logging every ounce of water. It means staying connected to how you feel. This guide helps you do that by giving you soft metrics to check in with—like energy, digestion, bloating, or clarity. You'll find spaces in the back to mark these things, not with numbers, but with notes.

For example, if you notice that the pink salt trick gives you more regular digestion, you might also notice that your skin starts to look clearer. If you skip a few days and start feeling sluggish, it won't be about guilt—it will just be a pattern you recognize. You'll have evidence, not rules. And that's powerful.

Let the Guide Work for You

There's a reason the word "guide" was chosen for this section. This book isn't a lecture. It's a partner. It walks with you through each stage of creating a more grounded, energized morning. You can use it in pieces or all at once. You can take it slow or go all in.

Whatever pace you choose, the guide is here to give you structure *without pressure*. It's a map, not a mandate. And if you use it consistently, even in a way that feels imperfect, you're going to feel the difference.

CHAPTER 1
What Is the Pink Salt Trick?

THE ORIGINS: FROM AYURVEDA TO TIKTOK

Long before it became a hashtag or a viral clip on your "For You" page, the pink salt trick had a story—one that stretches across continents and generations. While today it might appear as another wellness trend in pastel colors and curated glassware, its roots are much deeper than most people realize. This ritual wasn't born from social media. It was remembered there.

Let's rewind. Long before "gut health" became a mainstream term, ancient health systems were experimenting with natural ways to wake up the body, prepare it for digestion, and support internal balance. These traditions didn't have clinical trials or lab reports, but they had centuries of observation and practice. In places like India and Tibet, that knowledge became part of daily life—passed down through morning rituals, herbal combinations, and deeply intuitive self-care.

The Ayurvedic Foundation

In Ayurveda, the traditional health system of India dating back over 3,000 years, the morning is seen as a sacred window for resetting the body. There is a concept known as *dinacharya*, or "daily routine," which includes practices meant to align the body with natural rhythms. One such practice is the drinking of warm water, often infused with herbs or minerals, to stimulate digestion and cleanse the system.

Salt water—specifically a kind that contains trace minerals—was used to balance internal energy and kick-start the digestive fire, known as *agni*. Pink Himalayan salt, sourced from ancient sea beds near the base of the Himalayas, holds a place in this tradition due to its mineral content and grounding properties. Unlike table salt, which is heavily processed and often stripped of its minerals, pink salt is considered more "alive" in Ayurvedic terms—something closer to the natural elements of the earth.

Ayurveda never marketed itself as detox. Instead, it focused on supporting the systems already built into the body. The idea was never to shock your body into submission, but to gently guide it back into alignment—especially first thing in the morning, when the body is most sensitive and impressionable.

Traditional Chinese Medicine and Salt's Role

In Traditional Chinese Medicine (TCM), salt also carries symbolic and physical weight. It's associated with the kidney meridian, which governs water metabolism, adrenal function, and foundational energy. Salt is used sparingly but purposefully in both diet and remedies, especially during times of seasonal transition or fatigue.

Though pink salt itself isn't native to Chinese practices, the broader idea of using mineral salts to balance fluid levels and support internal harmony is well documented. In fact, one common TCM principle is that taste corresponds with organ function—and salt corresponds with the kidneys.

When used appropriately, salt is thought to strengthen the kidneys, improve clarity, and increase the body's capacity to handle stress.

These concepts might feel distant at first glance, but if you pause, they're closer than you think. Feeling foggy, depleted, or bloated? Traditional systems would ask how your hydration and mineral balance are affecting your energy—not how many steps you've taken or how many calories you've burned.

Enter the Wellness Revival

Fast forward a few thousand years, and suddenly we're seeing influencers talk about this same concept—sometimes knowingly, sometimes not. The pink salt trick as it's known today usually includes a glass of warm water, a pinch of pink salt, and sometimes lemon or apple cider vinegar. The wording may be different, the delivery more digital, but the underlying idea hasn't changed: start the day by supporting your body's natural systems rather than overriding them.

It's no accident that this revival happened when it did. In recent years, especially post-pandemic, more and more people—especially women—began questioning the fast-fix culture of wellness. The fatigue of counting, tracking, over-planning, and bouncing between "cleanses" and "cheat days" created space for something slower. The pink salt trick came in quietly. It didn't promise to change your life in a weekend. It just offered a glass of something that felt *right*.

And people noticed. A video demonstrating the trick might get hundreds of thousands of saves and comments like, "I've been doing this for a week and already feel less bloated," or "This is the only thing that's helped my morning headaches." Whether those comments are scientific proof is beside the point—the human experience has always been the first clue that something is worth exploring.

Why It Took Off on TikTok

There's a reason why this ritual landed so well on platforms like TikTok and Instagram. It's visual. It's easy. It fits into that five-second aesthetic that wellness content now requires. But here's the interesting part: it's also something you *feel* once you try it. That's what makes it sticky.

Many trends blow up for being flashy. The pink salt trick stuck because it's personal. Someone might try it because it looks cute on screen—but they keep doing it because it helps them feel less sluggish, less foggy, more in control. That's not something a filter can manufacture.

It also checked a lot of boxes that modern wellness seekers care about:

- Low cost—just water, salt, and maybe a lemon.
- No need for equipment—no blenders, no timers, no apps.
- Customizable—you can tweak the recipe without "messing it up."
- Based on natural ingredients—nothing synthetic or overly processed.
- Rooted in a larger conversation about gut health, hydration, and balance.

Suddenly, something ancient became brand new again. Not because it was changed, but because it was remembered.

Blending Ancient and Modern without Appropriation

There's a responsibility, too, when we bring ancient practices into modern wellness. It's easy to gloss over the roots or cherry-pick what looks trendy while forgetting the culture that cultivated it. That's why it matters to name these origins—not just to give credit, but to remind ourselves that wellness is not new. It's often a rediscovery of what previous generations already knew and practiced with care.

This book doesn't pretend to be a textbook on Ayurveda or Chinese medicine. But it does hold space for the idea that your body might know more than it's been allowed to express. That something as simple as salt, water, and attention could be a way of listening—not fixing.

WHY IT WORKS: HYDRATION, MINERALS, AND HORMONAL BALANCE

There's a reason so many women feel an almost instant shift when they start drinking the pink salt elixir in the morning. It's not just mental. The ingredients may seem simple—just salt and water, maybe a little lemon—but together, they support a trio of functions your body depends on every single day: hydration, mineral balance, and hormonal regulation. These systems are constantly working in the background, but they don't always get the support they need. The pink salt trick is like giving them a head start, before your day even begins.

Hydration That Actually Works

You've probably heard the advice: "Drink more water." It's everywhere. But what's missing from that message is how to actually *absorb* the water you drink. That's where salt comes in.

Plain water, while helpful, can sometimes move too quickly through your system without fully hydrating your cells—especially first thing in the morning when your electrolyte levels are low. Electrolytes are minerals that carry an electric charge and help your body regulate fluid balance, muscle contractions, and nerve signals. Sodium, one of the key electrolytes, plays a starring role here.

When you add a small amount of mineral-rich salt—like pink Himalayan salt—to your water, you're essentially creating a homemade electrolyte solution. It doesn't need to be complicated or sports drink-level salty. Just enough to help your cells hold onto the water instead of flushing it straight out.

Many women report that after drinking the pink salt elixir, they feel less dry, more alert, and more awake—not because they chugged a gallon of water, but because their body could actually *use* what they gave it.

The Morning Dehydration Window

Overnight, your body naturally loses water through breathing and sweating. By the time you wake up, you're already slightly dehydrated. If you go straight to coffee—which acts as a diuretic—you're compounding that loss. This can lead to:

- Headaches or brain fog
- Low energy and irritability
- Sluggish digestion
- Dull, dry skin

Starting your day with a mineralized hydration ritual helps reverse this trend. It sets a foundation for all your other systems to perform better—from digestion to circulation to mental clarity. And when those systems work better, you feel better without needing to overhaul your entire routine.

Minerals: The Underrated Powerhouses

Pink Himalayan salt is more than just pretty crystals. It contains trace amounts of minerals like calcium, potassium, magnesium, and iron—minerals your body needs to function properly but may not be getting enough of through diet alone.

Let's talk about magnesium, for example. It's involved in over 300 enzymatic reactions in the body, including those that regulate mood, muscle recovery, and sleep. A surprising number of people, especially women, are low in magnesium, which can show up as fatigue, poor sleep, and muscle cramps. While the amount of magnesium in pink salt is modest, using it daily can provide a small but consistent supplement to your intake.

Potassium helps with nerve function and blood pressure regulation. Calcium supports muscle function and bone strength. Even iron, though present in smaller amounts, plays a role in energy production. What matters here isn't just quantity—it's the synergy. These minerals work best when taken together, and pink salt offers them in a naturally balanced ratio.

You might be thinking, "But aren't we supposed to *limit* salt?" That's a valid concern—especially if your only exposure to salt has been the processed kind that's added to packaged foods. But there's a major difference between table salt (which is highly refined and often contains anti-caking agents) and natural salts like Himalayan salt, which are unrefined and mineral-rich.

Used in small, measured amounts—especially paired with water—pink salt doesn't "spike" your sodium intake. Instead, it supports electrolyte balance and keeps the body's systems running more smoothly. Think of it as a mineral tool, not a seasoning.

Hormonal Balance Starts with Stability

Now we reach the layer that often surprises people. How can a pinch of salt in a glass of water affect something as complex as hormones?

It starts with stress.

When your body is stressed, it releases cortisol—a hormone that helps you cope in the short term but can cause chaos if it stays elevated for too long. Cortisol affects your appetite, sleep, digestion, and even where your body stores fat. One of cortisol's biggest triggers? Dehydration and mineral imbalance.

When you're dehydrated—or when your sodium levels are too low—your adrenal glands (the ones that produce cortisol) have to work harder to maintain balance. This keeps your body in a subtle but persistent stress mode. You might feel this as fatigue that doesn't go away, sugar cravings, or a general sense of being "wired but tired."

Giving your body water *plus* minerals first thing in the morning helps regulate your adrenal response. It tells your system, "We're safe, we're nourished, we're okay." And from that calmer baseline, other hormones like insulin, ghrelin (your hunger signal), and leptin (your satiety signal) can function more smoothly.

There's also a link to digestion. When your digestive system works well—meaning food moves at the right pace, nutrients get absorbed, and inflammation stays low—your hormones don't have to work as hard to compensate. The pink salt elixir helps with all of this by priming your stomach acid, supporting hydration, and reducing bloating.

Real-World Feedback, Real Impact

Hundreds of women report feeling noticeable shifts within days of starting the pink salt ritual. Not dramatic changes, but steady improvements:

- Less bloating in the belly, especially in the morning
- More regular digestion, without relying on supplements
- Better skin texture, likely due to improved hydration
- Increased energy without needing an extra cup of coffee
- Less intense sugar cravings, especially in the late afternoon

These aren't promises—they're patterns. You may not feel *all* of them. But it's likely you'll feel *some*, especially if hydration, stress, or digestion are weak spots for you right now.

And unlike most "fixes," this one doesn't require perfection. If you skip a day, your body doesn't rebel. It just picks up where it left off.

WHAT MAKES IT DIFFERENT FROM OTHER "DETOX" TRENDS

If you've ever fallen into the rabbit hole of "quick fixes," you know the pattern. A new product promises to flush out toxins, melt belly fat, or restart your metabolism. It usually comes with a rigid plan, expensive ingredients, and some degree of suffering—hunger, restriction, or discomfort dressed up as discipline. And like clockwork, most of those plans leave you feeling disappointed, depleted, or worse: like you failed.

So when something like the pink salt trick shows up in the same conversation, it's fair to ask: isn't this just another detox trend in prettier packaging?

The answer is no—and understanding *why* requires a closer look at how this ritual works differently, both in philosophy and practice. Unlike other detox trends, the pink salt trick doesn't demand extreme shifts, rely on fear, or sell you a vision of health that only exists on filtered screens. It's grounded in simplicity, biology, and sustainability.

Not a Cleanse. A Ritual.

Many detox trends are built around the idea of deprivation. Juice cleanses, fasting apps, and liquid-only diets often market themselves as a reset—but what they're really asking for is removal. Remove sugar. Remove food. Remove your social life for a few days while you sip green liquids in isolation.

The pink salt ritual does the opposite. It starts your day with addition. You *add* minerals, *add* hydration, *add* a gentle moment for your body to prepare for the day ahead. It's not about flushing everything out—it's about giving your body what it's missing so it can function as it was designed to.

This isn't just language. The mindset shift is real. When your first act of the day is rooted in nourishment instead of restriction, it creates a ripple effect. You're less likely to binge later, less likely to chase energy with sugar or caffeine, and more likely to check in with how you feel rather than following a script.

Gentle on the Body—and the Mind

One of the defining traits of traditional detoxes is intensity. Think cayenne lemon water that burns going down, or charcoal drinks that taste like regret. Some trends go as far as including "emergency" colon flushes and harsh diuretics that leave you feeling drained and unsteady.

The pink salt trick? It's gentle. You drink it. That's it. There's no shocking the system. No lightheadedness. No long list of warnings. When used correctly, it supports your system rather than overwhelming it. The goal isn't to push your body harder—it's to make things work a little more smoothly.

And then there's the mental part. You don't have to schedule your life around this ritual. You don't need to cancel plans, skip meals, or explain to coworkers why you're drinking clay out of a mason jar. This is a habit that fits around your life, not one that demands your life rearrange around it.

No Expensive Products or Hype Machines

Another key difference? This ritual isn't selling you a product. You can walk into nearly any grocery store or even a gas station and find the ingredients you need. Pink Himalayan salt, water, and optionally lemon or apple cider vinegar—these aren't exclusive or secret. They're available to everyone.

Contrast that with most detox trends, which are tied to product lines. Detox teas, supplement kits, digital subscriptions with countdown timers—there's always a purchase involved. And often, those purchases lead to diminishing returns. You feel better for a few days (because you ate less or drank more water), but the moment you stop, everything slips back.

The pink salt trick doesn't rely on scarcity or branding. It's quiet. And that's part of what makes it powerful. It respects your autonomy. It lets you be the one in control.

No One Is Telling You to Be "Perfect"

A lot of detox programs come with unwritten rules about who they're for. If you've ever read a health plan and felt like it wasn't designed with you in mind, you're not alone. Many wellness trends assume you have hours of free time, an unlimited grocery budget, or no other responsibilities competing for your energy.

This one doesn't. It's a method that understands your mornings might include getting kids ready, fielding emails, or just trying to get your shoes on before the bus comes. And it meets you there. You can use it every day, or a few times a week. You can adjust the ingredients, the temperature, the timing. You don't "fail" this ritual if you miss a day.

There's also no deadline. No five-day boot camp or 10-day transformation. No before-and-after photos designed to create panic. Instead, you get to decide what success looks like. Maybe for you it's more energy. Maybe it's smoother digestion. Maybe it's just a few minutes of quiet where your body and mind can settle before the rest of the day starts.

The Results Come From Consistency, Not Shock

That's perhaps the biggest difference. Traditional detoxes operate on shock. Shock the system, drop some weight fast, and hope you can transition to maintenance before the rebound kicks in.

The pink salt trick relies on consistency. Small changes, repeated often. Supportive habits that compound over time. You might not notice much on day one, but give it a week, and the shifts become harder to ignore:

- Your stomach feels flatter in the morning
- Your cravings decrease around mid-afternoon
- Your sleep becomes a little deeper
- Your mood feels more steady

None of these happen overnight. But they do happen—and when they do, they don't come at the cost of your energy or your sanity.

It Honors the Body, Not Just the Trend Cycle

Finally, this ritual is different because it comes from a place of honoring the body, not fixing it. It doesn't start with the idea that you're broken. It doesn't suggest you need to be cleansed like a machine that's malfunctioned.

Instead, it assumes your body already knows how to detox, digest, and restore. It just needs the right inputs. And rather than reinventing the wheel, this ritual supports the systems you already have—your digestive tract, your kidneys, your adrenal glands.

That quiet respect is missing from most trends. And it's part of why the pink salt trick has stayed relevant—not just as a moment, but as a morning anchor for women looking for something real.

CHAPTER 2
The Core Recipe

THE PINK SALT MORNING ELIXIR: INGREDIENTS & STEP-BY-STEP PREP

If you've ever scrolled past a "morning wellness drink" online and thought, *That looks nice, but I have no time,* you're not alone. A big part of what makes the pink salt elixir different is that it's not just another fancy drink made for Instagram. It's practical, affordable, and designed to fit into real mornings—groggy, rushed, or otherwise.

This isn't a ceremonial routine that requires a yoga mat and perfect sunlight. It's a glass. A pinch. A pour. Maybe a slice of lemon, if you've got it. And yet, those small steps—done consistently—can kickstart hydration, digestion, and energy in a way that feels surprisingly noticeable.

Let's break down exactly what's in it, why each part matters, and how you can make it work even if your mornings are a bit chaotic.

What You'll Need

You don't need a shopping list or a health food store haul to get started. The base recipe calls for only two ingredients, plus one optional.

- High-quality pink Himalayan salt (fine grain)
- Filtered, warm water
- (Optional) Fresh lemon juice

Let's look at each of these a little more closely so you're not just doing the steps, but actually understanding what they're doing for your body.

Pink Himalayan Salt

This is the heart of the recipe. Unlike typical table salt, which is heavily refined and stripped of minerals, pink salt is naturally harvested and contains trace amounts of minerals like potassium, magnesium, calcium, and iron.

These minerals aren't just fancy additions—they're vital for how your body maintains hydration, nerve signaling, and muscle function. And in the morning, when your body is waking up after hours of no water intake, those minerals help your cells actually absorb the water you drink instead of flushing it right back out.

A little goes a long way. You're not trying to make salty water. You want just enough to lightly mineralize it without turning it into something you have to choke down.

Warm Filtered Water

This part isn't just a preference—it's purposeful. Warm water is gentler on your stomach first thing in the morning and supports the activation of your digestive system. Cold water can shock your gut when you're just waking up, while warm water helps nudge things along.

Filtered water is recommended because tap water can contain chlorine, fluoride, or metals that may interfere with the mineral balance you're trying to restore. That said, if filtered water isn't immediately available, don't let that stop you. The bigger win is consistency, not perfection.

Optional: Lemon Juice

If you have a lemon on hand and want to add a squeeze, it's a great bonus. Lemon juice helps stimulate stomach acid production, which can improve digestion throughout the day. It also adds a fresh, slightly tart flavor that can balance out the salt.

But this is optional. The base ritual still works without it, and some people with sensitive teeth or acid reflux prefer to skip the citrus.

Step-by-Step Prep Guide

Now, let's go through the actual steps. Feel free to adapt this depending on your routine, but here's the starting point that works for most people.

Step 1: Heat Your Water

You want your water to be warm—not boiling, not cold. Think of it like the temperature of tea that's sat for a few minutes. You can heat your water in a kettle, in the microwave, or just run warm tap water and let it sit.

Start with about 10 to 12 ounces of water. This amount is ideal for supporting hydration without overfilling your stomach.

Step 2: Add the Salt

Using a measuring spoon or your fingers, add about ⅛ teaspoon of fine pink Himalayan salt to the water. Stir well until it's fully dissolved. You should barely taste the salt—it should be subtle, not overwhelming.

Some people experiment with a slightly higher amount if they're sweating more (during workouts or hot weather), but it's best to start small and adjust slowly.

Step 3: Add Lemon (Optional)

If using lemon, squeeze about half a lemon's worth of juice (roughly one tablespoon) into the mixture. Stir again. You can use a fresh wedge or pre-squeezed juice, though fresh is ideal for the best flavor and vitamin C content.

Step 4: Sip Slowly

This isn't a shot—it's a sip. Try to drink the mixture over five to ten minutes, if possible. Use the time as a small window to focus, stretch, or just breathe before the rest of your day begins.

Even if you're getting kids ready or heading into traffic, this moment can feel grounding. Some people like to pair the drink with a bit of journaling or a light stretch. Others sip it while making breakfast. There's no perfect routine—just one that fits your life.

Small Adjustments for Real Mornings

Life isn't always predictable, so here are a few ways to keep the habit going even when you're in a rush or your kitchen looks like a tornado hit it.

- If you're traveling, pack a small bag of pink salt in your purse or suitcase and ask for hot water and lemon at a café or hotel.
- If you forget in the morning, it's still helpful to drink the elixir mid-morning. Just aim for an empty stomach for the best effect.
- Try prepping a lemon wedge the night before so your sleepy brain doesn't have to think too hard in the morning.
- If your mornings are too hectic, make it the first thing you do before coffee or emails—even if it's just one small glass.

Some readers keep a sticky note on the fridge or next to the coffee pot to remind them. Others make it part of a bigger morning ritual (which we'll explore later in this book). However you integrate it, the key is repetition. Small, simple, repeatable.

And when you do this consistently, you're not just giving your body minerals and hydration. You're telling it, "I've got you." And that message, repeated every day, starts to echo in ways that go far beyond salt and water.

FAQS: WHEN TO DRINK IT, ON AN EMPTY STOMACH, SAFETY, AND MORE

Once you've got the pink salt elixir recipe down, the next wave of questions usually comes fast. *Should I drink it before coffee? What if I skip a day? Can I take it while pregnant?* These aren't just random concerns—they reflect a real desire to understand how and when to use the ritual in a way that feels safe, supportive, and sustainable. Let's walk through the most common questions and give you clear, thoughtful answers grounded in how the body works and what real-life use looks like.

When Should I Drink the Pink Salt Elixir?

The most effective time to drink the elixir is right after waking up, on an empty stomach. That window—those first few moments before your body gets flooded with caffeine, food, or mental stimulation—is when your system is most responsive.

You've just spent 6 to 8 hours (hopefully) asleep, during which time your body has been slowly dehydrating. Even mild dehydration can lead to morning brain fog, fatigue, and slow digestion. Starting the day with mineralized warm water rehydrates you quickly and helps signal your body to begin digestive processes smoothly.

That said, this isn't a "do it or it won't work" situation. If you're the kind of person who wakes up starving, or if you take medication first thing with food, you can still use the elixir a bit later—just aim for a relatively empty stomach when possible. A 20- to 30-minute buffer between the drink and your first meal gives it a chance to do its work.

Some women also choose to drink it mid-morning if their mornings are too rushed. That's still supportive. This is about making it fit your life, not building your life around it.

Can I Have Coffee After?

Yes—just not *immediately* after.

Coffee is acidic and acts as a diuretic, meaning it increases the amount of fluid your body excretes. Drinking it too soon after the pink salt elixir can counteract some of the hydration benefits. A good rule of thumb is to wait 15 to 30 minutes between the salt drink and your first cup of coffee.

You might find that after a few days on this ritual, you actually *need* less coffee to feel awake. Some women notice a more stable energy curve, fewer caffeine crashes, and improved focus—all before their latte hits the mug.

Is It Okay to Drink Every Day?

Yes—when used properly, this ritual can be part of your daily wellness routine without concern. You're using a small amount of pink salt—about 1/8 teaspoon—in a full glass of water. That's well within a safe range for most healthy adults and provides trace minerals your body can actually use.

It's also worth noting that many people drastically *reduce* their intake of processed sodium when they start prioritizing whole foods and hydration. So for many, this salt addition is balancing rather than excessive.

That said, if you have a condition that affects your sodium levels—such as kidney disease, high blood pressure, or adrenal disorders—you should talk to your healthcare provider before adding any mineral supplement, including pink salt, to your routine.

Should I Avoid It If I'm Pregnant or Breastfeeding?

This is one of the most sensitive questions, and for good reason. During pregnancy and postpartum, your body is in a unique state with different needs and sensitivities. The general consensus is that mineralized hydration is not only safe but often helpful during these times—especially if you're struggling with fatigue, constipation, or low electrolyte levels.

However, every pregnancy is different. If you're pregnant or nursing and thinking about starting this ritual, here are a few things to consider:

- Use half the salt dose (start with a pinch) and see how your body responds.
- Keep the drink plain (skip lemon or vinegar if you have reflux or nausea).
- Hydration is especially important when breastfeeding, and this drink can be a gentle way to support that.

Always check with your provider, especially if you've been advised to monitor sodium intake or manage fluid retention.

Can Kids or Teens Drink It?

The short answer: not usually necessary, but not harmful in moderation. Children and teens typically don't need targeted electrolyte support unless they're recovering from illness or experiencing heavy physical activity. Their hydration needs are often met through water and food.

However, if a teen is showing interest in wellness and wants to participate in a morning ritual, a milder version (with just a pinch of pink salt and warm water) can be safe. Avoid overusing or treating it as a "weight loss" tool for minors. For them, hydration habits should be about energy and wellness—not control.

What If I Miss a Day?

Life happens. If you forget your elixir one morning, nothing breaks. This isn't a detox plan with a 7-day reset and rigid sequence. It's a gentle support tool. Your body won't backslide if you skip a day—or even a week.

Some readers find that after doing the ritual consistently, their body begins to remind them. They wake up thirsty, a little foggy, and they *want* the drink. That internal nudge is a great sign that your body has been responding to the habit.

If you've been off track, don't overthink your return. No need to "start over." Just begin again. The effects are cumulative, not calendar-based.

Can I Drink It Before a Workout?

Yes—and it can actually support your performance. The trace minerals in pink salt help regulate fluid balance, nerve conduction, and muscle contractions. This is especially helpful for women who experience lightheadedness or cramping during workouts.

Here's how to time it: drink your elixir about 30 minutes before your workout, especially if it's early in the day and you haven't eaten yet. You can follow it with a small pre-workout snack if needed.

If you're training later in the day, it's still helpful—but it doesn't need to be doubled. One serving in the morning is usually enough. If you sweat heavily or train in heat, consider adding another pinch of salt to your water bottle.

Is There Anyone Who Shouldn't Try This?

Most healthy adults can safely try the pink salt ritual. But there are a few exceptions:

- If you've been advised by a doctor to follow a low-sodium diet
- If you have uncontrolled high blood pressure or kidney issues
- If you take diuretics or medications that affect fluid/sodium balance

In these cases, check with your provider before adding any type of mineral supplementation—even small amounts like this. The goal is always to support the body, not to add unnecessary complexity or risk.

OPTIONAL ADD-INS: LEMON, GINGER, APPLE CIDER VINEGAR, HONEY

If the core pink salt elixir is the base outfit, then these optional add-ins are the accessories. They're not required—but the right one can change the whole feel of your morning ritual. Each of these ingredients has been used for generations in kitchens and wellness circles alike, not as fads, but as staples. They're common, versatile, and often already sitting in your pantry or fridge.

This part of the ritual is where you can make it yours. Whether you're someone who loves a bold, tangy flavor first thing in the morning or you prefer something softer and grounding, these additions can fine-tune the drink to suit both your taste and your body's needs. Let's explore what each one does, how to use it, and when it might be the right choice for you.

Lemon: The Classic Wake-Up Call

Of all the add-ins, lemon is probably the most well-known—and with good reason. It brings a clean, citrusy brightness to the drink that helps offset the mild saltiness. But lemon isn't just for flavor. It has real physiological effects that make it a natural partner to the elixir.

Lemon juice is rich in vitamin C, a key antioxidant that supports the immune system and helps with collagen production and iron absorption. But its impact goes beyond nutrients.

What It Does:

- Stimulates stomach acid, which improves digestion and the breakdown of food later in the day
- Acts as a mild diuretic, helping to flush the system in a gentle way
- Supports bile production from the liver, aiding in fat digestion
- Balances the taste of the elixir with acidity

For many people, just half a lemon (about one tablespoon of juice) is enough to feel the difference. If you experience acid reflux or have sensitive teeth, you may want to dilute it further or skip it entirely on certain days.

Some readers squeeze fresh lemon the night before and store it in the fridge to save time in the morning. That way, they're not scrambling for a citrus knife while half-awake.

Ginger: The Digestive Booster

Fresh ginger root doesn't just taste great—it has a long history of use in herbal medicine, particularly in Chinese and Ayurvedic traditions. It's warming, grounding, and particularly helpful if your digestion tends to be sluggish or irregular.

You don't need much. A small slice, grated or steeped in hot water before you add the salt, can bring a little fire to the ritual—in a good way. Ginger can support movement in the gut, reduce nausea, and even ease cramping.

What It Does:

- Helps stimulate digestion and reduce bloating
- Improves circulation, which is great if you feel cold in the morning
- Has natural anti-inflammatory properties
- Gives the drink a warming kick that can replace the need for early caffeine

Some prefer to make a "ginger shot" style elixir by blending lemon and ginger together first, then adding warm water and salt. If that sounds too intense, try steeping thin ginger slices in hot water for a few minutes before mixing them in.

Ginger also pairs beautifully with a teaspoon of honey if you're feeling under the weather. Just keep in mind it's potent, and too much can make the drink feel spicy on an empty stomach.

Apple Cider Vinegar (ACV): For Blood Sugar and Bloating

Apple cider vinegar has a distinct tang—and a bit of a reputation. For some, it's a magic bullet. For others, it's a bit much first thing in the morning. The truth is somewhere in the middle: ACV has benefits, but it needs to be used with care and awareness.

The kind of vinegar you want is raw and unfiltered, ideally with the "mother" intact. That's the cloudy sediment at the bottom of the bottle, filled with enzymes and beneficial bacteria.

What It Does:

- May help balance blood sugar levels when consumed before meals
- Supports digestion by boosting stomach acid, similar to lemon
- Helps reduce bloating, especially for those who feel heavy in the belly after waking up
- Acts as a gentle detoxifier for the liver

A half to one teaspoon is usually enough. Too much can cause burning or nausea, especially on an empty stomach. Always dilute well with warm water, and if you're trying it for the first time, start with less than you think you need.

You might also choose to alternate ACV and lemon on different mornings to give your system variety and see which feels better.

Honey: The Soothing Sweetener

Honey is the most surprising of the optional ingredients. Most people don't associate "sweet" with a health ritual—but a small amount of raw honey can actually support your body in specific ways, particularly if you need quick energy or immune support.

We're not talking about supermarket squeeze bottles here. The best honey is raw and local, with minimal processing and all the enzymes intact.

What It Does:

- Provides a quick source of natural sugar to gently lift blood sugar without a crash
- Has antimicrobial and antibacterial properties
- Can soothe the throat and support respiratory health
- Pairs well with lemon and ginger for a "wellness tonic" effect

If your mornings tend to start slow—especially if you wake up groggy or lightheaded—a half teaspoon of honey in your elixir may help balance things out.

That said, if your goal is fasting or lowering sugar intake, it's okay to skip it. The beauty of this ritual is that it's customizable, and nothing is mandatory.

Finding Your Flavor and Function Combo

Here's where the magic happens. Once you understand what each ingredient offers, you can start to build a version of the elixir that's uniquely yours. Try out one add-in at a time for a few days. Notice how you feel. Then adjust.

Some combinations readers love:

- Lemon + Ginger (for digestion and energy)
- ACV + Lemon (for bloating and blood sugar control)
- Lemon + Honey (for immunity and gentler mornings)
- Ginger + Honey (for sore throats or winter mornings)

Try not to overcomplicate it. The goal isn't to create a superdrink with every add-in under the sun—it's to support your body where it's asking for help. Think of these additions as intuitive tweaks rather than required steps.

And if one morning all you have time for is water and salt, you're still doing the most important part. Everything else is just fine-tuning.

CHAPTER 3

The Science Behind the Sip

HOW PINK SALT AFFECTS DIGESTION, BLOATING, AND CRAVINGS

Let's be honest—many of us don't pay much attention to how digestion works until something feels off. Bloating after meals, irregular bowel movements, or those 4 p.m. cravings that seem to hijack your brain—these might feel random, but they usually point to an underlying imbalance in how your body is processing food and managing energy. And here's where something as simple as pink salt in warm water, first thing in the morning, can start shifting the picture.

No, pink salt isn't magic. But its mineral makeup, combined with hydration, can support three major systems that most people—especially women in high-stress, high-responsibility lives—are struggling to regulate: digestion, bloating, and cravings. When these start working more smoothly, everything else—from energy to mood to motivation—follows.

Let's Start with Digestion

When you hear the word digestion, it's easy to think of food breaking down in your stomach. But digestion actually begins before the first bite. It starts with signals. The pink salt elixir plays a role in jumpstarting those early signals by activating receptors in your mouth and stomach, which cue your digestive system to prepare for incoming food.

Warm water helps by relaxing the stomach muscles and gently waking up the gut. Salt, particularly unrefined pink salt, triggers the release of saliva and gastric juices. That includes hydrochloric acid (HCl), which is what your stomach needs to properly break down proteins and absorb nutrients.

Many women unknowingly suffer from low stomach acid, not high. Symptoms like bloating, heaviness after meals, and nutrient deficiencies (especially iron and B12) are often tied to underproduction of acid, not overproduction. Starting your day with a small amount of pink salt and warm water helps stimulate your stomach's natural processes before food even enters the equation.

There's also the impact on the gallbladder. Saltwater, especially with a squeeze of lemon or a dash of apple cider vinegar, can help promote bile flow. Bile isn't just for digesting fat—it's also how your liver gets rid of toxins. If bile isn't flowing well, digestion slows down and you may experience constipation, greasy stools, or that uncomfortable "brick in the belly" feeling.

Reducing Bloating—Without Cutting Out Entire Food Groups

Bloating is one of the most common complaints women have about their gut. It's uncomfortable, unpredictable, and often leads to restrictive eating patterns. But here's the thing: bloating isn't always about what you eat. Often, it's about *how* your body is able to process and move what you've eaten.

Pink salt supports hydration and electrolyte balance, which are both vital for regular, efficient bowel movements. When your body is slightly dehydrated—even just a little—it can lead to constipation and slow transit time in the gut. That backed-up feeling, paired with fermentation in the colon, creates pressure and swelling.

Drinking the elixir in the morning does two things:
- It rehydrates your system after 6–8 hours of no water
- It provides sodium, which helps your cells retain and use that hydration effectively

Many people mistakenly think they're bloated because of food sensitivity, when in reality, they're not absorbing water well or digesting slowly due to low stomach acid. When you address those two issues—hydration and digestion—you give your body the chance to work the way it was built to.

The result? Bloating goes down, waistlines feel lighter, and the uncomfortable "puffiness" that tends to set in by midmorning or late afternoon becomes a rare visitor instead of a daily routine.

Tackling Cravings at Their Source

Now let's talk about cravings. Sugar cravings, salty snack cravings, "just one bite" of chocolate that turns into the whole bar—most of these have nothing to do with willpower. They're usually signals from the body trying to get something it's missing.

Mineral imbalances are one of the most overlooked causes of cravings. If your body is low on sodium, magnesium, potassium, or calcium, it might push you toward salty or sweet foods in an attempt to correct the imbalance. That's why cravings can feel so intense—it's not just in your head. Your body is speaking. And often, it's saying, "I need support."

By starting the day with a small mineral dose from pink salt, you may find that your cravings reduce—sometimes dramatically. Not because you're full. Not because you're distracted. But because your body got what it needed early, so it doesn't have to sound the alarm later.

It's worth noting that stress and blood sugar crashes also play a big role in cravings. And both of those are impacted by hydration and electrolyte status. When your cortisol is high or your insulin is spiking and crashing, your body starts looking for fast comfort—usually sugar or caffeine. But when you hydrate well, support your adrenals with minerals, and start the day with stability, those frantic signals start to quiet down.

The Gut-Brain Connection: Why It All Feels So Emotional

There's another layer to all of this that often gets missed: your digestive system doesn't just manage food—it talks to your brain. This is called the gut-brain axis. And when your gut is stressed, inflamed, or sluggish, it affects how you think, feel, and even behave.

Minerals like magnesium and sodium help regulate the nervous system. Pink salt doesn't have large amounts of magnesium, but the overall effect of mineralized hydration can be calming to the system. For some, that shows up as less anxiety. For others, it's fewer mood swings tied to blood sugar fluctuations. Either way, it's one more reason why this ritual can feel supportive even if you can't always explain why.

If you've ever felt hangry, overwhelmed, or inexplicably foggy, this could be a sign that your body is struggling with internal signals—and those signals often start with digestion.

Real Stories, Real Feedback

A growing number of women report that after a week of using the pink salt trick, they feel less inflamed, less snack-driven, and more comfortable in their own skin. Here's what some describe:
- "I'm not rushing to grab something sweet after lunch anymore."

- "My pants fit better, but more importantly, I feel like I'm not carrying extra water weight all the time."
- "My belly doesn't hurt after dinner like it used to."
- "I used to think I needed probiotics and enzymes. Turns out, I just needed better hydration and salt in the morning."

Of course, every body is different. This ritual won't fix everything. But it can be a reset point—a way to support the systems your body relies on, without restriction or rules. And when digestion, bloating, and cravings aren't dominating your day, you have space to focus on what actually matters.

REAL NUTRIENT FUNCTIONS (EXPLAINED SIMPLY)

When people hear the word *minerals,* their eyes tend to glaze over. It sounds scientific, abstract—something from a nutrition textbook, not something that actually affects your energy, focus, or how your jeans fit. But the truth is, these tiny nutrients are doing big work every single day inside your body. And when they're out of balance, you feel it.

Pink Himalayan salt contains trace amounts of several of these nutrients—namely sodium, potassium, calcium, magnesium, and iron. These aren't just names on a supplement bottle. They're players in your body's electrical system. And no, that's not just a metaphor. Your body literally runs on electric signals. Your heartbeat, muscle contractions, nerve messages, even the way you digest food—these processes rely on the movement of charged particles called electrolytes. That's where these minerals come in.

Let's break each one down in real-life terms. No jargon. No medical degrees required.

Sodium: Not the Villain You've Been Told

Sodium tends to get a bad rap. We've been told to avoid it, cut it, fear it. And yes—too much processed sodium from packaged foods can be a problem, especially for people with certain health conditions. But that's not what we're talking about here.

The sodium in pink salt isn't the same as the stuff in fast food fries or microwave meals. It's not processed, bleached, or chemically treated. In small amounts, it helps your body stay hydrated, keeps your blood pressure stable, and supports nerve and muscle function.

What you may not know is that when you sweat, exercise, or even just go through a stressful day, your body loses sodium. If you don't replace it, you might feel lightheaded, tired, or unusually irritable. Some women even mistake it for low blood sugar.

That's why adding a pinch of pink salt to your water in the morning can make such a difference. You're not "loading up" on salt—you're restoring balance after a long night without fluids.

Potassium: The Calm-Down Mineral

Potassium is like the chill friend in your mineral crew. It balances out sodium, helps regulate your heartbeat, and supports muscle relaxation. Without enough of it, you might feel anxious, wired, or twitchy. Sound familiar?

Most people don't get enough potassium in their diet. Processed foods are typically low in it, and while fruits and vegetables help, even those aren't enough if your body is under stress or you're sweating a lot.

While pink salt contains only a small amount of potassium, every bit counts—especially if you're starting the day dehydrated or hormonally imbalanced. When paired with potassium-rich foods (like bananas, leafy greens, or avocado), you're giving your body tools to stay steady and responsive, not reactive and frazzled.

Magnesium: The Quiet Workhorse

If there's a mineral most women are low in—and that makes a noticeable difference when corrected—it's magnesium.

Magnesium is involved in hundreds of processes in the body, but let's keep it simple. It:

- Helps relax your muscles (including the ones in your digestive tract)
- Supports deep sleep and lowers stress hormones like cortisol
- Assists in the metabolism of carbohydrates, protein, and fats
- Plays a role in blood sugar regulation and energy production

Low magnesium can show up as cramps, restless legs, insomnia, irritability, or sugar cravings. The kind of magnesium found in pink salt is minimal, but it's part of a bigger support system. Think of it like setting the stage: you're not relying on pink salt alone for your magnesium needs, but you are creating the right conditions for your body to hold on to the magnesium it *does* get from your diet.

And for many women juggling work, kids, hormones, and a sleep-deprived brain, that little shift can feel like a lifesaver.

Calcium: More Than Just Bones

Calcium is famous for bone health—and yes, it's vital for that. But it also helps your muscles contract, supports heartbeat regulation, and assists in transmitting messages between your brain and body.

If your calcium levels are off, you might experience numbness, tingling, or even brain fog. Some women notice more intense PMS symptoms or difficulty focusing. And here's the interesting part: calcium works best in the presence of magnesium. They balance each other.

Pink salt contains small amounts of natural calcium, giving your body a trace amount to work with first thing in the morning. Again, it's not a calcium supplement—but it's part of a bigger support system that helps keep your internal signals running smoothly.

Iron: The Energy Spark

Iron doesn't actually give you energy—but try living without enough of it and you'll understand its importance fast. It helps transport oxygen throughout your body. No oxygen = no energy.

Many women, especially those who menstruate, are chronically low in iron. Fatigue, pale skin, hair thinning, and cold hands or feet can all be signs of low iron levels.

The trace iron in pink salt is minimal but bioavailable—meaning your body can recognize and use it more easily than some synthetic forms. It's not enough to replace iron-rich foods like red meat or legumes, but it adds a gentle layer of support that can be especially helpful if you're already doing other things to improve your iron intake.

The Trace Mineral Team

Beyond the "big five" (sodium, potassium, magnesium, calcium, iron), pink Himalayan salt contains dozens of trace minerals—zinc, phosphorus, iodine, selenium, and others. These don't get as much press, but they still matter. They help regulate thyroid function, support skin health, balance hormones, and assist in detoxification pathways.

Think of it like seasoning for your internal systems. It's not about mega-dosing—just adding subtle, steady support.

Why Natural Sources Matter

One reason pink salt works well for this ritual is that the minerals come in natural balance. Unlike supplements, which deliver isolated nutrients in high doses, natural mineral sources offer trace amounts in a form your body is more likely to recognize and use.

It's like the difference between eating an orange and taking a vitamin C tablet. The orange comes with fiber, flavonoids, and enzymes that help your body absorb the vitamin C more effectively. Same idea here.

That's why the elixir isn't about chasing numbers or hitting percentages. It's about providing your body with what it needs to *start the day working*—instead of playing catch-up.

THE TRUTH ABOUT SALT AND WEIGHT LOSS

If you've spent any time trying to lose weight, you've probably been told to cut back on salt. It's one of those recommendations that shows up on lists right next to "drink more water" and "move your body more." And like a lot of advice in the wellness space, it's based on a kernel of truth—but oversimplified, misunderstood, and often misused.

So, let's pause. Let's talk about what salt actually does in your body, why it's been blamed for weight gain and water retention, and why the right kind of salt—used in the right way—can actually support your metabolism, not sabotage it.

This isn't about flipping the script just to be edgy. It's about getting honest with how your body works, so you're not stuck bouncing between low-salt rules and rebound bloat.

Where the Fear of Salt Came From

Most of the fear around salt traces back to one thing: sodium. High sodium intake has long been linked to high blood pressure and heart disease. And while that connection is valid in certain situations, the broader context often gets left out.

Most Americans get their sodium from ultra-processed foods—think chips, canned soups, deli meats, and frozen dinners. It's not the salt shaker at the dinner table that's the problem. It's the hidden, excessive sodium in convenience foods that don't offer any nutritional balance.

This is where the nuance comes in. Pink Himalayan salt, unlike processed table salt or the additives in packaged foods, contains not only sodium but also trace minerals that help the body absorb and balance that sodium more effectively. It's a different experience for your body.

So when you add a small amount of pink salt to warm water first thing in the morning, you're not feeding the same cycle that creates inflammation and water retention. You're actually helping your body *release* excess water and improve internal balance.

Water Weight vs. Fat Storage

Let's clear this up right now: salt doesn't cause fat gain. If you eat a salty meal and wake up puffy the next day, that's not fat. It's water.

Your body holds onto water for lots of reasons—stress, hormones, lack of sleep, processed food, and yes, poor hydration. Ironically, not drinking enough water or avoiding all salt can *increase* water retention. Your body gets nervous, thinks it's in a state of drought, and starts clinging to every drop.

Now, enter the pink salt ritual. A glass of warm water with natural salt in the morning does a few things:

- Rehydrates you after hours of sleep with no fluid intake
- Provides electrolytes that help your cells absorb and hold onto water in a balanced way
- Encourages your kidneys and lymphatic system to release stored water that's no longer needed
- Supports adrenal function, which affects how your body handles stress and fluid balance

So while it might seem odd to *add* salt to lose water, it actually works. And over time, that reduced bloat can mean flatter stomachs, less puffiness in your face and hands, and more comfortable clothes—all without ever touching a scale.

The Metabolic Connection

Salt also plays a quiet, under-discussed role in metabolism. Your thyroid, adrenal glands, and kidneys all use sodium and other electrolytes to function properly.

Your thyroid, in particular, needs iodine—a mineral that's often added to table salt but not always absorbed well. Pink salt contains trace amounts of iodine and other minerals like selenium and iron that support thyroid health. If your thyroid is sluggish, your metabolism may be too. Supporting it gently—through food, hydration, and minerals—can help reset how your body burns fuel.

The adrenal glands, which sit on top of your kidneys, are responsible for producing hormones like cortisol and aldosterone. These hormones regulate fluid balance, energy, and stress responses. When your adrenals are depleted (which happens easily in high-stress lifestyles), you may crave salt, feel dizzy when standing, or feel wiped out after minor effort.

A small amount of pink salt in the morning can help your adrenals recover, reducing stress-related weight gain and helping your body feel more stable overall.

But What About Blood Pressure?

Yes, it's true—excess sodium in the diet can raise blood pressure. But context matters.

In clinical settings, that concern is usually tied to sodium from processed food, not from whole, mineral-rich sources. If you're already on a low-sodium plan for a medical reason, of course, follow your provider's advice. But if your health is stable and you're using a modest amount of pink salt in water—not shaking it over every meal—you're unlikely to push your sodium intake into dangerous territory.

In fact, some women notice their blood pressure stabilizes when they start hydrating better and replacing key electrolytes. Dehydration, not salt, is often the hidden trigger for dizziness, fatigue, and even blood pressure spikes.

The key is balance. You're not dumping salt into your diet—you're using it intentionally, in small amounts, to support processes that are already happening in your body.

Weight Loss Without Extremes

One of the most common patterns in dieting is over-correction. Cut all carbs. Cut all salt. Cut all joy. Then swing in the opposite direction when your body rebels.

The pink salt ritual doesn't ask you to eliminate anything. It's not about deprivation. It's about support.

When you start your day with hydration, minerals, and a few minutes of stillness, you're more likely to:

- Eat balanced meals because your cravings are reduced
- Feel more in tune with your hunger cues
- Experience fewer energy dips and crashes
- Have better digestion and less bloating

All of those factors support weight loss—not by fighting your body, but by working with it. And maybe that's the biggest shift of all. This isn't a hack or a shortcut. It's a reminder that your body wants to feel good. You just need to give it the right inputs.

CHAPTER 4
THE 21-DAY PINK SALT RITUAL PLAN

HOW TO BUILD A DAILY WELLNESS HABIT

If there's one thing most people agree on, it's this: starting something is easy. Sticking with it? That's the hard part. Whether it's going to the gym, eating more greens, or yes—drinking warm salt water in the morning—consistency is where results live. But consistency doesn't have to mean perfection, and building a daily wellness habit isn't about discipline alone. It's about design.

Let's look at how to turn the Pink Salt Trick from a good idea into something you actually do. Every day. Without forcing it. Without guilt-tripping yourself. And without making your mornings feel like a checklist of tasks that only a wellness influencer could love.

First, Redefine What a "Habit" Looks Like

Most of us imagine habits as these locked-in, automatic things—like brushing your teeth or making coffee. You do them without thinking. But habits don't have to be rigid. They can be fluid. They can shift with your mood, your cycle, your kids' schedule, or your job. What matters is that the core *action* stays present.

The goal here isn't to build a flawless, military-style morning ritual. It's to create a low-resistance starting point. Something you can do groggy-eyed, in your robe, before your brain starts listing all the day's to-dos.

So, what's the real job of this ritual? It's not to "burn fat" or "detox" or chase numbers on a scale. It's to wake your body gently, support your hydration, and set a tone of care that follows you through the rest of the day.

When you think of it like that, the pressure drops—and the habit becomes easier to keep.

The "Anchor Habit" Approach

One of the simplest ways to build a new habit is to attach it to something you're already doing. These are called anchor habits. You don't have to reinvent your whole morning. You just plug the pink salt elixir into a slot that already exists.

Here are some real-life examples:

- Drink your elixir right after brushing your teeth.
- Make it the first thing you do after waking your kids up.
- Set it on your nightstand and drink it before you check your phone.
- Combine it with your gratitude practice or journal time.

The key here is making it predictable. Not forced. Not perfect. Just "this comes after that." Your brain loves patterns. Give it one.

Preparation = Fewer Excuses

One of the top reasons people skip their morning ritual? They're not prepared. It sounds obvious, but if you're digging around your kitchen in the dark looking for lemon and a clean glass, your habit becomes harder than it needs to be.

Here's how to prep for success:

- Keep a small jar of pink salt in a spot you see every morning.
- Pre-cut lemon slices or store lemon juice in a sealed container in the fridge.
- Use the same glass or bottle each day—make it a visual cue.
- Fill your kettle or water filter the night before to save steps in the morning.

Removing friction is one of the most powerful ways to keep a habit alive. The easier it is to start, the more likely you are to stick with it—even on messy mornings.

Habit Tracking (But Keep It Light)

Tracking your habit can reinforce the behavior—but only if it feels encouraging, not punishing. You're not trying to be a machine here. You're building trust with yourself.

Consider keeping a simple visual tracker: a calendar with check marks, a sticky note on the fridge, or a quick entry in your Notes app. You're just saying, "Yes, I showed up today." Even if the rest of your day feels like chaos, that moment still happened.

Bonus: seeing a streak of check marks can build momentum. Humans are wired to keep going when we feel progress, no matter how small.

When You Miss a Day (Because You Will)

Missing a day doesn't break the habit. Quitting does. One of the fastest ways to sabotage your wellness practice is to think you have to "start over" every time life happens.

Instead of judging yourself, ask a better question: *What made this hard today?* Maybe you overslept. Maybe you traveled. Maybe your toddler melted down before you had a chance to boil water.

These aren't failures—they're feedback. Use that feedback to tweak the setup. Maybe that means prepping the night before. Maybe it means traveling with a salt packet in your bag. Maybe it means dropping the lemon on days when you're just trying to get out the door.

Flexibility keeps the habit alive. Rigidity kills it.

Habits That Feel Good Last Longer

Another key to long-term habits? They have to feel good. Not just in theory, but in your actual body.

After a week or two of using the pink salt ritual, many women report things like:

- "My stomach feels calmer in the morning."
- "I don't crash mid-morning like I used to."
- "I feel hydrated before I even pour my coffee."
- "It's my moment of peace before the day starts."

That's the reward loop kicking in. When your body starts linking the ritual to feeling better, the motivation to keep going gets stronger. You're no longer doing it because a book told you to—you're doing it because your body asked for it.

Build Around Your Season, Not Someone Else's

Here's one last truth: your habits will look different depending on the season of life you're in. What works in your 30s with young kids may look different in your 40s with an empty nest. Winter routines don't always match summer ones. Stressful work weeks need a different rhythm than lazy weekends.

And that's okay.

The beauty of a daily wellness habit is that it adapts to you—not the other way around. The pink salt ritual isn't a rule. It's a rhythm. And once it's in place, it supports you without demanding perfection.

Certainly! Here's the section based on your exact instructions:

WEEK-BY-WEEK FOCUS (HYDRATION → DIGESTION → ENERGY BOOST)

Establishing a daily wellness habit is a great start—but what happens after that first cup of salty warm water? How do you build momentum without burning out? The answer lies in structure, not intensity. That's where the 21-Day Pink Salt Ritual Plan comes in.

Instead of trying to do everything at once, this plan guides your body—and your mind—through a progressive shift. Each week has a specific focus. These focuses are not random. They're designed to work with your body's natural rhythms, giving you time to adjust, observe, and respond. Think of it as tuning an instrument: one string at a time.

Week 1: Hydration Reset

Let's be honest—most people walk around mildly dehydrated and don't even know it. You might assume that hydration means drinking more water, but it's not that simple. The key isn't just fluid intake—it's absorption. Without the right minerals, especially sodium and potassium, water can pass right through you without actually reaching your cells.

In this first week, your job isn't to overhaul your life. It's to build a single, consistent morning habit: drink the pink salt elixir.

That small act helps your body:

- Rehydrate after 6–8 hours of fluid loss during sleep
- Trigger digestive enzymes and gut motility to prep for the day
- Begin balancing electrolytes for steadier energy levels

You may notice early changes like fewer headaches, reduced morning fatigue, or even improved mood. If you're someone who usually feels "off" until your second cup of coffee, this week might surprise you.

You don't need to change your diet yet. Just observe how your body responds to better hydration. Keep track of subtle shifts—bloating, skin, thirst cues. Week 1 is about listening.

Week 2: Digestion Support

Now that your body is hydrated and receiving trace minerals daily, it's ready to go deeper. In Week 2, the focus moves to digestion—not in a restrictive, diet-obsessed way, but in a supportive one.

This is where you might start to refine your meals slightly. Think less about calories, more about how food feels. Does it sit well? Do you feel sluggish after eating? Or energized?

To support digestion this week:

- Continue your morning elixir daily
- Add gentle digestive aids if needed (like lemon or ginger in your drink)
- Eat slowly and mindfully at meals
- Notice post-meal symptoms like gas, bloating, or cravings

This isn't about cutting food groups. It's about learning your rhythm. Maybe lunch feels better when it's lighter. Maybe dinner is where you need more grounding foods. Keep notes—not rules.

Many women notice that their appetite begins to regulate naturally around this time. Mid-morning or late-night cravings may decrease. You might also experience more regular bowel movements, less brain fog, and clearer skin. All of this is digestion working better—not because you're restricting, but because your system is more supported.

Week 3: Energy + Rhythm

By Week 3, you've built momentum. You're hydrated. Your digestion is humming along. Now it's time to tune into energy—not the jittery kind you chase with coffee or sugar, but the stable, lasting kind that makes you feel capable and calm at the same time.

This week, you'll use the pink salt ritual as an anchor—not just to start your day, but to check in with your energy flow.

Ask yourself:

- When do I feel the most clear and focused?
- When do I crash, and why?
- Which meals or snacks give me energy, and which ones leave me dragging?
- How does movement affect my mood and focus?

This is the week to layer in gentle movement, if you haven't already. A 10-minute stretch, a short walk after meals, or a few yoga poses can amplify the effects of everything you've already built.

It's also the perfect time to shift your mindset. Up until now, the habit might've felt new or experimental. But by Week 3, many people describe it as something they look forward to. It's no longer a task—it's a ritual. A moment of peace. A signal that you're starting the day on your terms.

If you hit a plateau here, that's okay. It doesn't mean the plan isn't working. It usually means your body is adjusting again, recalibrating. Energy changes don't always show up as fireworks—they show up as steadiness. Less crashing. More ease.

Why This Order Works

Hydration, digestion, energy. It sounds simple, but it follows your biology. When your cells are hydrated, your digestive system wakes up. When your digestion is smoother, your blood sugar is steadier. When your blood sugar is steady, your energy is consistent. And when your energy is consistent, your choices reflect that. That's where sustainable change begins—not with willpower, but with physiology.

The 21-Day Pink Salt Ritual Plan isn't about outcomes. It's about process. You're not being asked to follow a diet, track macros, or perform for a before-and-after photo. You're being asked to show up—to your glass of water, to your breath, to your morning—and to keep showing up.

TROUBLESHOOTING COMMON ISSUES (CRAVINGS, HEADACHES, FATIGUE)

Even with the best intentions, wellness plans rarely go off without a hitch. You could be doing everything "right"—drinking your morning elixir, keeping your meals clean, following the 21-day structure—and still find yourself staring into the fridge late at night, battling a headache before noon, or dragging your feet through the day with no energy to spare. This doesn't mean you've failed. It just means your body is communicating.

These hiccups aren't signs to give up. They're invitations to slow down, observe, and adjust. Let's walk through the most common issues people experience while building the Pink Salt Ritual habit—why they happen, and what you can do about them.

Cravings: Not Just About Willpower

Let's start with the one that sparks the most guilt: cravings. Sugar, carbs, salt, caffeine—whatever your craving looks like, it often feels like a loss of control. But cravings are never random. They're messages from the body, not character flaws.

If you're getting intense cravings during this plan, ask yourself:

- Am I under-eating during the day?
- Is my sleep quality disrupted?
- Did I skip the salt elixir or hydrate poorly today?
- Am I stressed, bored, or emotionally tapped out?

Cravings often spike when your blood sugar dips. That's especially common in the late afternoon (think 3 to 5 p.m.), when your energy naturally ebbs. If your meals are too light, too rushed, or missing quality protein and fat, your body may nudge you toward a "quick fix" like chocolate or chips.

The Pink Salt Ritual can help here—when used strategically. If you feel a craving coming on, sip a glass of water with a pinch of salt and a splash of lemon first. Wait five minutes. This combo can often stabilize the signal before you act on the impulse.

Also: don't underestimate emotional cravings. If you're dealing with a tough day, it's okay to acknowledge that food feels like comfort. But ask: *Is this what my body needs, or what my mood wants?* Sometimes, simply naming the difference gives you space to make a different choice.

Headaches: What's Actually Going On?

Headaches are another common complaint during the first week of this ritual. They're frustrating, especially if you started this process to feel better—not worse. But here's what's likely happening: your body is adjusting.

Salt affects hydration at the cellular level. If you've been chronically dehydrated (many of us are), your cells may be rebalancing fluid. This can cause a temporary shift in blood volume or even blood pressure, leading to mild tension or throbbing in the head.

It's also worth asking:

- Have you cut back on caffeine or sugar recently?
- Are you eating enough throughout the day?
- Is your salt intake consistent—or sporadic?

To reduce headaches:

- Make sure you're drinking water gradually, not all at once.
- Eat something with protein or healthy fat in the morning—don't skip meals.
- Consider adding a magnesium-rich food (like pumpkin seeds or leafy greens) to your day. Magnesium and sodium work together in the body.
- Don't go overboard with the salt. More is not better. Follow the measured recipe.

If headaches persist for more than a few days or become severe, always check with your healthcare provider. But mild, short-term tension often signals that your system is recalibrating—and that's not always a bad thing.

Fatigue: A Surprising Side Effect

It might sound odd to feel more tired during a wellness plan that's supposed to energize you. But for many people, fatigue shows up early—and for good reason.

If you've been running on stress hormones (think: caffeine, deadlines, sleep debt, high cortisol), your body may interpret the shift in rhythm as a signal to finally rest. The Pink Salt Ritual rehydrates your cells and supports adrenal balance. That process can trigger a temporary "let down" effect where you feel more tired before you feel better.

Think of it like finally taking off a backpack you didn't realize you were carrying. Once it's off, you suddenly feel the weight you've been holding.

Here's how to support your body through that reset:

- Go to bed 30 minutes earlier—even if you don't feel exhausted yet.
- Keep your morning routine consistent, even on weekends. The ritual matters.
- Eat enough. Under-eating is a major cause of energy crashes.
- Limit caffeine after 1 p.m. so your sleep cycle isn't disrupted.
- Prioritize protein at every meal. It stabilizes blood sugar and improves stamina.

Fatigue isn't always a problem to solve—it's often a cue to rest. Listen to it. Your energy will return, but it will be cleaner, steadier, and less dependent on external stimulants.

When to Adjust—and When to Pause

If you're experiencing more than one of these symptoms, don't panic. You're not doing anything wrong. But it may be time to make a small adjustment.

Try this:

- Use a little less salt for a day or two, especially if you're experiencing bloating or headaches.
- Add a second glass of plain water mid-morning to improve hydration.
- Simplify your meals—aim for clean proteins, vegetables, and healthy fats.
- Make your morning ritual shorter if time stress is affecting your energy.

If things feel consistently worse after five to seven days, it's okay to pause. That doesn't mean you're quitting. It means you're respecting your body's limits. Come back when you feel ready—or when life gives you the bandwidth to re-engage.

This plan isn't a challenge. It's a tool. You don't "win" by suffering through it. You benefit by using it with awareness.

CHAPTER 5
THE PINK SALT-FRIENDLY MEAL BLUEPRINT

FOODS THAT COMPLEMENT THE TRICK (ANTI-INFLAMMATORY & LIGHT)

Your pink salt elixir is the spark—now it's time to fuel the fire. What you eat during the rest of your day can either support the benefits of the Pink Salt Trick or quietly undo them. The goal isn't to follow a rigid meal plan. It's to make intentional food choices that match the gentle, grounding nature of the ritual itself.

You don't need a special diet to do this. You don't need to count anything. Instead, you'll lean into foods that reduce inflammation, support digestion, and provide lasting energy without weighing you down. Light doesn't mean unsatisfying. And anti-inflammatory doesn't mean boring. You'll see how these choices are more about clarity than control.

The Power of Anti-Inflammatory Foods

Inflammation isn't always bad. It's part of how your body heals. But chronic, low-grade inflammation—the kind linked to bloating, fatigue, joint stiffness, and stubborn weight—tends to simmer beneath the surface when your diet is heavy on processed foods, added sugars, and industrial oils.

When you combine pink salt with meals that fight inflammation, you give your body a chance to reset. You're not forcing change. You're removing the noise so your system can function the way it's meant to.

Some everyday anti-inflammatory foods that pair beautifully with your morning ritual:

- Leafy greens (spinach, arugula, kale) for minerals and fiber
- Fatty fish (like wild salmon or sardines) for omega-3s
- Blueberries, raspberries, and cherries for antioxidants and natural sweetness
- Extra virgin olive oil as your go-to fat for cooking and drizzling
- Avocados for fiber and healthy fats that keep you full
- Herbs and spices (turmeric, ginger, rosemary) for their subtle but powerful effects

You don't need to overhaul your pantry. Start by crowding in these foods. Let them take up more space on your plate. Slowly, the heavier stuff gets pushed out—not by restriction, but by nourishment.

Light Eating Doesn't Mean Less Food

Let's talk about "light." It's a word that's been used to sell us diet products and low-fat labels. But in this context, light refers to how food feels in your body—not how few calories it has.

A light meal is one that gives you energy, not brain fog. It doesn't leave you hungry an hour later, but it also doesn't make you want to lie down immediately after eating. Think clean proteins, roasted or raw veggies, healthy fats, and slow carbs—especially when you're easing into a new rhythm.

This might look like:
- Scrambled eggs with arugula and olive oil on the side
- A smoothie with avocado, berries, chia seeds, and a pinch of salt
- Quinoa with roasted zucchini, grilled chicken, and tahini drizzle
- Lentil soup with turmeric and lemon, paired with a side salad

It's not about being "low" anything. It's about being intentional.

Light also means minimizing ingredients that cause stress in the body—especially during digestion. For some, that means avoiding processed dairy, refined sugar, or fried foods. For others, it means skipping the mid-afternoon ultra-sweet latte. The key is paying attention to how you feel after eating—not just how it tastes going down.

Timing and Pairing Matter

Your morning ritual sets the tone, but what follows still matters. A pink salt elixir hydrates and stimulates digestion. To keep that momentum going, the next thing you put in your body should complement—not clash—with that effect.

Here are a few strategies to build on your morning start:
- Don't eat immediately after the elixir. Give your body 20–30 minutes to fully process it.
- Break your fast with something easy to digest—smoothies, eggs, soups, or warm cooked vegetables work well.
- Use your first full meal to add in the anti-inflammatory powerhouses: greens, olive oil, fatty fish, herbs, seeds.
- Stay light at lunch if you're working or mentally focused—think clean proteins and fiber, without heavy sauces or starchy overloads.
- If you're snacking, go for function—not just flavor. Apple slices with almond butter, olives, or roasted chickpeas can keep blood sugar stable and cravings low.

Dinner is where you can anchor down. That doesn't mean binge. It means relax into warmth—think brothy soups, stir-fried vegetables, or baked salmon with sweet potato. No spreadsheets, no macros—just grounded nourishment.

Don't Forget Pleasure

One of the biggest mistakes in wellness culture is the idea that healthy food must be bland. That's a recipe for rebellion. If your meals feel like punishment, your body will push back—often through cravings, fatigue, or mental burnout.

So yes—season your food. Use pink salt on roasted carrots. Squeeze lemon over steamed greens. Toss chopped herbs into everything. Explore spices like cumin, coriander, or smoked paprika. Let your food smell amazing, look vibrant, and taste satisfying.

When you eat food that looks alive, you feel more alive. It's not a coincidence. Your nervous system responds to color, texture, and aroma. That's not "extra." That's part of the ritual too.

WHAT TO AVOID (WITHOUT RESTRICTIVE DIETING)

Let's be clear—this isn't about cutting out everything that brings you joy. The last thing you need is another food list that makes you feel guilty every time you open the fridge. But if you're doing the Pink Salt Trick to feel lighter, more energized, and more in tune with your body, some foods are simply going to work *against* you. It's not about being restrictive—it's about being selective.

You don't need to ban entire food groups or label things as "good" or "bad." What matters is noticing what foods tend to leave you feeling bloated, tired, sluggish, or craving more junk an hour later. That awareness alone can help you naturally avoid the things that slow your progress—without the drama of dieting.

The Sneaky Energy Thieves

Some foods drain your energy not because they're inherently evil, but because of the way they interact with your hormones, digestion, and blood sugar. If your goal is sustainable wellness—not just a short detox—then dialing back these common culprits can make all the difference:

- Refined sugar and syrupy sweeteners (especially in "healthy" drinks and yogurts)
- Highly processed carbs like white bread, crackers, or pastries
- Industrial oils (canola, soybean, corn) used in many restaurant and packaged foods
- Deep-fried snacks, even in small quantities—your gut notices
- Artificial sweeteners that may trick your taste buds but confuse your metabolism
- Sodium-heavy packaged meals that crowd out real minerals with bloating salt forms

Are these foods always "bad"? No. But if you're waking up feeling puffy, can't seem to shake cravings, or crash mid-afternoon, they might be behind the curtain pulling the strings.

Overeating Healthy Food Is Still Overeating

One of the biggest traps in wellness culture is assuming that if a food is "clean," you can have as much as you want. That's how you end up with three tablespoons of almond butter when you only needed one—or a giant green smoothie so packed with add-ins it might as well be dessert.

Instead of obsessing over portion sizes, pay attention to *satisfaction*. The Pink Salt Trick already helps regulate hunger signals by balancing hydration and mineral intake. But that only works if you're not constantly overwhelming your body with more than it asked for.

If you're feeling full but still eating "just because," that's worth noticing—not punishing yourself over.

Emotional Eating in Disguise

Sometimes, we eat things not because we're hungry, but because we're *tired, bored, anxious, or annoyed*. Sound familiar? That late-night bag of chips might be a signal that your stress levels—not your sodium levels—need some attention.

The goal isn't to eliminate all comfort foods. It's to *pause* long enough to ask: "Is this what I really want—or is this just a reaction?"

If you're constantly reaching for snacks that make you feel heavy afterward, it might be time to introduce a different form of comfort—one that doesn't come in a crinkly wrapper.

Gentle Awareness Over Harsh Rules

Here's the mindset shift: instead of asking "What can't I eat?", ask "What helps me feel clear, light, and grounded?" Then notice what pulls you away from that.

You don't need to label pizza or a glass of wine as mistakes. You just need to notice how your body feels after. And the more you practice this, the more naturally you'll start gravitating toward foods that support—not sabotage—your wellness.

Here are a few ways to create guardrails without turning them into cages:
- Don't keep trigger foods at home. If you have to leave the house to get it, you're more likely to pause and ask if you really want it.
- Decide ahead of time what foods are worth it for you. Not every treat needs to be eaten "just because it's there."
- If you do indulge, do it with intention. Eat it slowly. Savor it. And then move on—no spiraling, no over-correcting.
- Make your meals so satisfying that you're not chasing flavor highs later. That's what anti-inflammatory + delicious looks like.

It's Not All or Nothing

You're not failing if you eat chips one day or skip a homemade meal for takeout. But if it becomes the default, that's when the Pink Salt Trick loses its power to shift your baseline. This method works best when your whole lifestyle gently tilts toward balance—not perfection.

There will be travel days, celebrations, and PMS moments. That's real life. The key is having a rhythm to return to, not rigid rules that make you feel defeated after a slip.

In short: the trick isn't just about what you *do*—it's also about what you *don't need* anymore. And when you tune into that, you'll naturally find yourself avoiding the foods that dull your glow—not because you "shouldn't" eat them, but because you don't *want* to.

SAMPLE DAILY EATING RHYTHM (NO COUNTING, NO TRACKING)

Let's be honest—if calorie counting, macro tracking, and food diary apps actually worked long-term for most people, we wouldn't still be searching for something that feels simple, sustainable, and good. That's exactly why this chapter focuses on a gentle, nourishing rhythm that supports the Pink Salt Trick without forcing you into a spreadsheet every time you eat. This isn't about following a rigid plan. It's about creating a flow that's light, realistic, and deeply aligned with your natural appetite and energy shifts throughout the day.

At this point, you already know the Pink Salt Elixir sets the tone each morning. So the rest of your eating rhythm should feel just as purposeful—but without overthinking it. This chapter gives you a real-world structure to follow, one that supports hydration, stable energy, and reduced cravings.

Why Rhythms Matter More Than Rules

When you shift your focus from rigid food rules to consistent rhythms, you give your body something it truly loves: predictability. Our systems—digestive, hormonal, and metabolic—respond well to patterns. They thrive when meals come at regular intervals and when ingredients support rather than stress the system. Think of this daily eating rhythm not as a diet plan, but as a steady drumbeat. When it's in sync, everything else—from your energy levels to your mood—tends to follow suit.

That said, this rhythm doesn't require you to be perfect. Life happens. Travel, work shifts, social events—none of that disqualifies you from feeling good. The idea here is to come back to your natural flow whenever possible.

Your Core Eating Flow: Morning to Evening

The following structure is designed to pair naturally with the Pink Salt Trick. It's light on rules and rich in intention. You'll find that each section builds on the one before it—just like your body builds on each earlier cue to shape the rest of your day.

Morning

The moment you wake up, hydration is your priority. That's where the Pink Salt Elixir comes in—it's your first signal to your body that nourishment is on the way, but that digestion doesn't have to sprint.

About 20 to 30 minutes after the elixir, when your body feels ready for solid food, keep things simple:

- Focus on foods that are easy to digest—think smoothies, chia pudding, fresh fruit, or lightly cooked oats.
- Limit heavy proteins or fried items early on, which may stall digestion and lead to sluggishness.
- Consider warm drinks like herbal tea or hot lemon water to maintain that calming tone in your gut.

What you're doing here is layering hydration with gentle nourishment. You're not skipping meals or "fasting," per se—you're just asking your body what it wants first, and letting your morning foods be supporting players, not heavy hitters.

Midday

By lunchtime, your digestive fire (what Ayurvedic tradition calls "agni") is strongest. This is the ideal window for your most substantial meal of the day. That doesn't mean it needs to be oversized—it just means this is the time when your body is best equipped to process and assimilate a wide range of nutrients.

- Build your plate around vegetables first—steamed, roasted, or raw, depending on the season and your preference.
- Add in a clean protein source, like grilled chicken, lentils, eggs, or tofu.
- Include a healthy fat, such as avocado, tahini, olive oil, or seeds, to support satiety and hormonal balance.
- If you enjoy grains, go for a modest serving of something whole and minimally processed—quinoa, brown rice, or farro work beautifully.

The goal here isn't to eat until you're stuffed. It's to feel satisfied, grounded, and fueled for the second half of your day.

Afternoon

This is the time when energy typically dips—and so do blood sugar levels, which often trigger cravings for sugar, caffeine, or salt. Rather than white-knuckling your way through it or grabbing the first snack bar in sight, be prepared with light, hydrating support.

- Herbal teas (like peppermint, fennel, or dandelion) can help ease digestive stagnation.
- A small snack that combines fiber and fat—like a few slices of apple with almond butter, or cucumber rounds with hummus—can stabilize energy without spiking blood sugar.
- If you're feeling sleepy, step outside or move your body instead of reaching for coffee.

Remember, snacks are not cheats—they're tools. But the key is to use them with intention, not impulse.

Evening

Dinner should be your lightest main meal, especially if you tend to experience bloating or poor sleep. By evening, your digestive system starts winding down. Heavier foods eaten too late tend to sit in the gut overnight, disrupting rest and possibly leaving you with puffiness the next morning.

- Opt for broth-based soups, lightly sautéed vegetables, or simple stir-fries with gentle proteins.
- Avoid large amounts of dairy, red meat, or anything ultra-processed after sunset.
- Try to eat at least 2 to 3 hours before bed to give your body time to digest before sleep.

If you're still hungry later in the evening, choose something soft and digestible—like a banana, herbal tea, or a small handful of soaked almonds.

What You're Teaching Your Body

This rhythm is more than a structure—it's a quiet, daily practice of nourishment that helps your body and brain feel safe. And when your system feels safe, it stops holding on to inflammation, excess water weight, and those stubborn stress-driven cravings.

You're teaching your body that food is not scarce, that nourishment comes regularly, and that there is no need to overreact. It's not about being "good" or "clean"—it's about being consistent. And yes, you'll mess up sometimes. That doesn't cancel out the progress. Just return to the rhythm as often as you can.

What makes this rhythm special is that it's made for real life. You don't need a scale. You don't need a macro chart. And you definitely don't need a guilt trip. All you need is a bit of intention, a dash of curiosity, and a willingness to reconnect to what your body already knows: it likes rhythm. It likes flow. And it likes feeling good.

CHAPTER 6
DRINK & SNACK RECIPES FOR WELLNESS SUPPORT

DETOX WATERS WITH PINK SALT

If the words "detox water" make you think of a sad spa pitcher with three floating cucumber slices, we're about to change that. Pink salt detox waters are not about aesthetics or gimmicks—they're about gentle, daily support for your body's real systems. No wild promises, no liquid diets, and absolutely no starving. Just smart hydration paired with natural mineral balance. So let's walk through what these drinks actually do, why pink salt plays a key role, and how you can use them to feel better—not deprived.

The Real Point of a Detox Water (It's Not What You Think)

Forget about the idea that you can drink something and magically flush out "toxins" like it's some internal power-washing service. Your body already has detox systems: your liver, kidneys, lymphatic system, and skin. The problem is, modern life doesn't always support those systems. Between processed foods, stress, and dehydration, your natural detox pathways get sluggish.

That's where these waters come in. They're not miracle workers—but they're helpful. When you hydrate with a pink salt blend, you're giving your body something it actually recognizes: water with trace minerals that support digestion, circulation, and cellular activity.

Pink salt contains over 80 trace elements. Some of the most relevant here are magnesium (for muscle relaxation and better bowel movements), potassium (for fluid balance and nerve function), and calcium (not just for bones, but also muscle contractions and enzyme function). In small, consistent doses—especially in the morning or early afternoon—these minerals gently encourage your body to move things along: food, fluid, and, yes, bloating.

Why Plain Water Sometimes Isn't Enough

If you've ever chugged three glasses of plain water and still felt bloated or thirsty, it's not your imagination. Pure H2O doesn't always make it into your cells efficiently, especially if you're low on minerals. That's where a small pinch of pink salt makes a difference. The sodium in the salt helps carry water into your cells, which is why these detox waters can be more hydrating than plain water alone.

Here's another angle: if you're someone who often feels a mid-morning slump, has tension headaches, or tends to snack out of thirst instead of hunger, mineralized water can shift that pattern. You're not just drinking—you're absorbing.

When to Drink It and How Often

Let's get practical. Timing can really affect how your body responds to these drinks. Here's a rhythm that works for most people:

- **Morning:** Start your day with a tall glass of detox water before breakfast. It kickstarts digestion and helps flush out any fluid retention from sleep.
- **Mid-morning or pre-lunch:** If you feel a dip in energy, go for a second round—especially if you're someone who skips breakfast or delays meals.
- **Post-exercise:** A great time to replenish electrolytes naturally without a neon-colored sports drink.

You don't need gallons. One to three glasses spaced through the day is enough. Listen to your body—some days you might crave more, others less.

Ingredient Combos That Actually Work

Here's where things get fun. Pink salt is your base, but the combinations you build around it can change depending on your needs or taste. These aren't just about flavor—they each offer a little extra support depending on how you're feeling.

1. Lemon + Pink Salt

The classic. Lemon adds vitamin C, which supports collagen and immunity, and its slight acidity can stimulate digestive juices. This combo is especially helpful if you feel puffy or slow in the mornings.

2. Cucumber + Mint + Pink Salt

Cucumber hydrates and cools, mint soothes digestion, and together they're perfect for hot days or post-bloating recovery. This one is ideal after a salty meal or when your gut feels off balance.

3. Apple Cider Vinegar + Pink Salt + Cinnamon Stick

A more intense flavor but surprisingly energizing. ACV may support blood sugar stability and digestion, while cinnamon adds warmth and helps curb sugar cravings. This mix is a favorite around 3 p.m.—when most people reach for a snack they don't actually need.

4. Ginger Slices + Lime + Pink Salt

For anyone prone to nausea, motion sickness, or sluggish digestion, ginger is a go-to. Lime adds brightness and an antioxidant boost. If your stomach feels tight, or your digestion is "meh," this is a powerful little reset in a glass.

Tips to Make It Stick (Without Turning It Into a Chore)

You don't need to measure every sprinkle or buy a glass carafe to make this work. But a few small tricks can help make it part of your real routine:

- Keep a mason jar with a lid near your kettle or fridge—easy to prep the night before.
- If mornings are chaotic, set a reminder on your phone: "Hydrate kindly." Not "drink your salt water." Language matters.
- Batch prep: Mix your base water + salt in the morning, then pour into two or three bottles. Add lemon, cucumber, or herbs when ready to drink.
- Rotate your ingredients. Not for performance—but for enjoyment. If you look forward to the flavor, you'll be more consistent.

Who Should Be Cautious?

Let's talk boundaries. While pink salt detox waters are generally safe, they're not for everyone in every situation. If you're on a sodium-restricted diet, have high blood pressure, or take medications that affect fluid balance, talk to your doctor. That doesn't mean you can't ever try them—it just means the pink salt part might need to be reduced or skipped.

Also, more is not better. A pinch—think 1/8 teaspoon or just enough to slightly taste—is all you need in a liter of water. If the drink tastes too salty, it probably is. Your body doesn't need brine, it needs support.

Final Thought (Without Summing It All Up)

This isn't about selling you on another morning trend. It's about reconnecting with what your body already does—and giving it a little smarter support. Pink salt detox waters don't fix everything. But when you pair them with good sleep, steady meals, and low-pressure movement, they become part of a rhythm that feels a lot like balance. And that's more than enough.

NATURAL ELECTROLYTE BLENDS FOR ENERGY

You don't have to be a marathon runner to need electrolytes. That's one of the biggest misconceptions around hydration. You can be sitting at your desk, under the hum of artificial lights and air conditioning, and still find yourself tired, foggy-headed, or craving something salty—not because you're hungry, but because your body is low on what it needs to function: minerals and hydration that actually reach your cells.

That's where natural electrolyte blends come in. These are not flashy sports drinks with neon colors and long ingredient lists. They're simple, potent combinations you can make at home—designed to replenish and energize without stimulants, sugar spikes, or caffeine crashes.

Why Electrolytes Matter (Even If You're Not Breaking a Sweat)

Electrolytes are minerals like sodium, potassium, calcium, and magnesium that help your body manage fluid levels, nerve function, and muscle contractions. But they're also directly tied to how alert and energetic you feel. When you're even slightly dehydrated—or missing the mineral balance to absorb water properly—you'll feel it. That afternoon slump? It might not be about food or sleep. It could be your cells just asking for minerals.

The problem is that most people drink water and think they're doing enough. But water alone doesn't always hydrate—you need the right balance of minerals to help it actually move into your cells. That's the beauty of a well-made electrolyte drink: it makes hydration *work*.

Why Pink Salt Is the MVP

Himalayan pink salt is far more than a pretty crystal on a trendy restaurant table. Unlike regular table salt, which is stripped down and sometimes contains anti-caking agents, pink salt is rich in trace minerals. We're talking about over 80 naturally occurring elements like potassium, calcium, magnesium, and yes—sodium—all in a form your body recognizes.

A pinch of this salt in your drink gives you a micro-dose of these minerals and helps your body retain water in a balanced way—not in a bloating, uncomfortable way. It's about giving your system tools to hydrate *efficiently*, not just hold onto water like a sponge.

The Blueprint for a Natural Electrolyte Blend

Making your own electrolyte drink at home isn't just easy—it's empowering. You don't need powders or packets. You need a few real ingredients, and you're ready to go.

- *Filtered or spring water*
- *A pinch of pink Himalayan salt*
- *A natural acid: lemon juice or raw apple cider vinegar*
- *A touch of sugar from nature: raw honey or maple syrup*
- *Optional mineral boosters: coconut water, cucumber juice, herbal infusions*

This combination creates the perfect environment for water absorption—balancing sodium, potassium, and glucose just enough to help water get inside your cells, where it counts.

Morning Energy Kick Recipe

Here's one of the simplest and most reliable recipes for when you wake up feeling foggy or low-energy.

- 16 oz (about 500 ml) warm water
- Juice of ½ a fresh lemon
- ¼ teaspoon pink salt
- 1 teaspoon raw honey (or 1 tablespoon coconut water)

Stir until dissolved and sip slowly. Many people describe it as feeling like an "internal shower"—not dramatic, but a noticeable mental and physical boost within 10 minutes.

Matching Electrolytes to Your Day

What's great about these blends is how versatile they are. You can tweak ingredients based on your needs and the time of day. Some examples:

Mid-Afternoon Reset:

- Cold water with lime slices, a pinch of pink salt, fresh mint, and a teaspoon of coconut sugar.

After a Workout:

- 1 cup coconut water
- 1 cup filtered water
- A pinch of pink salt
- 1 teaspoon fresh ginger juice

Late Afternoon Drag:

- Warm water with a splash of apple cider vinegar, pink salt, a dash of cinnamon, and a teaspoon of raw honey. This blend supports digestion and wakes up your system gently.

Do They Really Work?

Studies published in the *Journal of the International Society of Sports Nutrition* have shown that electrolyte drinks with the right sodium-to-potassium ratio can help maintain mental clarity and physical endurance—even in non-athletes. Translation: these drinks aren't just for people lifting weights. They're for moms, creatives, professionals, and anyone who finds themselves running on empty halfway through the day.

In fact, many women who use the Pink Salt Trick report that these blends have replaced their second coffee. And once they make the switch, they rarely go back.

Pro Tip: Use Herbal Teas as a Base

Not everyone loves the slightly salty taste—especially first thing in the morning. If that's you, try using herbal teas as your base liquid. They add flavor, function, and a gentler overall taste.

Some favorites:

- Cold chamomile tea with lemon juice and pink salt
- Hibiscus tea with honey and cucumber juice
- Fennel tea with green apple juice and a dash of cinnamon

These combinations hydrate, nourish, and gently support your digestion and focus, without relying on caffeine or synthetic additives.

GUT-LOVING SMOOTHIES & SATISFYING SIPS

There's something undeniably comforting about sipping a smoothie that's both delicious and secretly good for your digestive system. But in a world overflowing with wellness trends, it's easy to get lost between probiotic powders, "superfood" lists, and gut microbiome buzzwords. So let's cut through the noise. This chapter is all about real, gut-loving smoothies and drinks—blended with purpose, guided by flavor, and supported by research that actually makes sense. No lab coats, no complicated elixirs. Just simple, tasty drinks that support your digestion and leave you feeling satisfied, not stuffed.

Why Focus on the Gut?

Your gut isn't just about digestion—it's a complex network of bacteria, hormones, enzymes, and neurotransmitters. It influences how your body absorbs nutrients, how often you crave sugar, and even how clear-headed or moody you feel. Some researchers now call the gut the "second brain," and not just for dramatic effect. Over 90% of the body's serotonin—a key player in mood regulation—is produced in the gut.

And yet, when your gut is out of balance, you feel it. Bloating, sluggishness after meals, erratic energy levels, and skin flare-ups can all trace back to digestive imbalance. The right kind of drink—packed with whole, raw ingredients that support digestion—can offer gentle, daily support for all of that without requiring a supplement drawer or a rigid schedule.

The Role of Smoothies in Gut Health

Smoothies offer a powerful tool for digestive health, not because they're "magic," but because they provide:

- Soluble fiber that helps bulk up stool and feed beneficial gut bacteria
- Hydration, which supports the movement of food through your system
- Enzymes from raw fruits and vegetables that support natural breakdown of food
- Room for fermented ingredients like kefir or yogurt without having to "eat" a bowl of it

But not all smoothies are created equal. Many commercial blends (and trendy Instagram recipes) are overloaded with sweeteners—natural or not—and miss the mark when it comes to what the gut really needs: balance. Fiber, fat, acid, and a bit of sugar in the right ratio—not a frozen fruit sugar bomb.

The Pink Salt Connection

Why include pink salt in gut-friendly smoothies or sips? Beyond taste, pink salt contains trace minerals that support hydration and can stimulate digestive processes, particularly when paired with acidic ingredients like lemon or fermented yogurt. A tiny pinch—literally—can help your body better absorb fluids, making your smoothie not just more flavorful, but more functional.

Ingredients That Matter (and Why)

Let's break down a few go-to ingredients that can truly make a difference for your digestive health:

Avocado

Rich in fiber and healthy fats, avocado helps slow digestion just enough to make absorption more complete. It also gives smoothies a luxurious, creamy texture without the need for dairy or bananas.

Kefir or Unsweetened Yogurt

These fermented dairy products are loaded with live cultures that replenish your gut with beneficial bacteria. While not all probiotics survive the digestive tract, kefir tends to contain resilient strains that can actually take root in the intestines.

Pineapple

More than just a tropical sweetener, pineapple contains bromelain, a natural enzyme that helps break down protein. This can ease post-meal bloating and support smoother digestion when included in smoothies.

Ginger

Ginger is one of the oldest known remedies for nausea, stomach upset, and bloating. It works as a natural prokinetic—meaning it helps "move things along" in your gut. A small knob peeled and blended can subtly heat your smoothie while calming your stomach.

Chia Seeds

Chia seeds expand in liquid, forming a gel-like texture that acts like a scrub brush through your intestines. They're especially helpful for those dealing with sluggish digestion or irregularity.

Cucumber

Hydrating, cooling, and low in sugar, cucumber works well in savory smoothies or lighter green blends. It's gentle on the stomach and high in water content—great for keeping things moving through your digestive system.

Sample Gut-Loving Smoothie Recipe: "The Calm Belly Blend"

- ½ avocado
- 1 cup unsweetened kefir
- ½ cup pineapple chunks (fresh or frozen)
- 1 teaspoon chia seeds (pre-soaked for 10 minutes in a splash of water)
- Small piece of fresh ginger (peeled)
- Pinch of pink salt

- Optional: ½ cup cold water or coconut water to adjust consistency

Blend all ingredients until smooth. Drink slowly. You might be surprised how full you feel without needing to finish the entire glass in one go.

Satisfying Sips That Aren't Smoothies

Not in the mood for something thick? There are plenty of gut-friendly options beyond smoothies that still feel indulgent.

Apple Cider Vinegar & Lemon Water

A simple mix of warm water, a tablespoon of ACV, lemon juice, and a pinch of pink salt can wake up your digestion in the morning. The acidity supports stomach acid production—especially helpful if you've felt bloated after eating lately.

Herbal "Digestive Tonics"

Try a cooled brew of peppermint tea, fennel seeds, and chamomile. These herbs help relax your digestive tract and reduce gas buildup. A splash of aloe juice or coconut water adds a smooth finish and keeps the drink from tasting too "earthy."

Cucumber-Mint Elixir

Blend cucumber with water, a handful of mint, and a small squeeze of lime. Strain if desired. It's refreshing, supportive of fluid retention, and great on a warm day when your digestion tends to slow down.

Tips for Making These Drinks Part of Your Routine

- Drink slowly—gulping anything, even a gut-friendly smoothie, can lead to bloating.
- Don't overload ingredients. Keep recipes simple so your digestive system doesn't get overwhelmed.
- Listen to your body. If you feel overly full, adjust portion sizes or ingredients the next day.
- Enjoy as a light breakfast or between meals—not immediately after a heavy lunch or dinner.

Gut-friendly drinks aren't meant to replace food, meals, or actual medical care—but they can offer everyday support that's gentle and surprisingly powerful. And when paired with something as simple as pink salt, they also help you stay hydrated and grounded, not just full.

CHAPTER 7

THE 5-MINUTE MORNING RITUAL THAT CHANGES EVERYTHING

DRINK WITH INTENTION

There's a moment each morning—brief, quiet, often overlooked—that can shift the tone of your entire day. Before texts buzz in, before emails stack up, and before your to-do list swallows your attention, there's the first sip. This chapter is about transforming that simple act into something powerful: not through effort, but through awareness. Because when you drink with intention, even something as humble as your pink salt elixir becomes more than hydration. It becomes a habit anchor, a daily act of care, and a reset for both body and mindset.

More Than a Morning Drink

Let's be honest: the pink salt elixir isn't magic. It's water, minerals, maybe lemon or ginger—simple ingredients. But simplicity is its strength. In a culture of overcomplicated rituals and 12-step routines, choosing to drink something functional and focused the moment you wake up is like saying, "I know what I need, and I'm going to start my day by giving it to myself."

The point isn't the pink salt. It's the presence. That's what separates a wellness habit from a wellness performance. You're not chugging this drink in front of a mirror while checking your hair or posting a "healthy morning" snap. You're doing it quietly. Eyes still soft. Maybe standing barefoot in your kitchen. And if that feels indulgent or strange, you're probably overdue for this kind of stillness.

Why Intention Works (and Science Backs It)

Drinking with intention isn't some vague spiritual trend. It's supported by how your brain works. The act of setting a brief internal cue—"I'm nourishing myself"—shifts how your brain processes the event. That kind of mindful behavior activates your parasympathetic nervous system, which is responsible for digestion, calm, and focus. It counterbalances the cortisol spikes that can otherwise start firing the moment your alarm rings.

In short: when you pause and mean it, your nervous system listens.

This is the exact opposite of gulping coffee while reading yesterday's emails or skipping breakfast only to snack all afternoon. Drinking with intention helps regulate your nervous system, which in turn helps regulate your appetite, mood, and even inflammation levels throughout the day.

What It Looks Like in Practice

There's no single way to "do" this. In fact, the more tailored and personal it feels, the more likely it is to stick. But if you're wondering how to build intention into your first sips of the day, here's what that might look like:

- Wake up and rinse your face or brush your teeth—whatever helps you feel physically awake.
- Prepare your morning elixir: pink salt in warm water, with optional lemon or ACV.
- Hold the glass. Pause. Take a breath.
- Think a simple thought: "This is for my energy." Or "This is how I take care of myself."
- Sip slowly. Not like medicine, not like a smoothie—just as a gesture of calm entry into the day.

You might stand near a window. You might sit. You might close your eyes. What matters is that your attention is on the drink, not your phone or your inbox.

The Psychology of Ritual

There's a reason high-performing athletes, CEOs, and creatives swear by rituals. Not because the ritual itself changes the world, but because it stabilizes their inner world. A five-minute routine gives structure where there's chaos, control where there's unpredictability. When your brain knows what comes next—wake, hydrate, center—it stops wasting energy on doubt and resistance.

It's not just about motivation. It's about clarity. When you start the day with something that's for *you*, not the world, you send a powerful signal: I matter. My needs come first, even if just for five minutes.

But What If Mornings Are Chaotic?

Good question. And valid. Not every reader has a calm kitchen or uninterrupted mornings. Kids, work, partners, noise—life doesn't always leave space for long rituals. That's why this one is designed to be short and adaptable.

Your pink salt elixir doesn't require incense or quiet. Just your focus for a moment. Even if you're sipping it while packing lunches or answering a toddler's questions, you can still think: "This is for me." You can still exhale between sips. That's enough. That counts.

And if you miss a morning? That's fine too. This isn't about perfection. It's about building a relationship with yourself that feels kind and steady.

What Makes This Different From Other Morning Hacks

You've probably tried a few "morning hacks" before. Cold showers. Breathwork. Journaling. Green powders. Maybe they worked, maybe they didn't. But what sets this habit apart is its simplicity and sustainability. You're not adding a new item to your checklist—you're just changing the *way* you do something you were already going to do: drink.

That's what makes it sticky. You already drink water in the morning. This just gives it meaning. And from there, that meaning begins to ripple out—into your food choices, your posture, your mood.

It's a Pause, Not a Fix

Let's not pretend this will "solve" your stress, your digestive issues, or your to-do list. It won't. But what it will do is create a buffer. A micro-pause. A moment when you check in instead of checking out.

And over time, those moments add up.

You start to crave them. You start to need less noise in the morning. You might even find that five minutes stretches into ten—not because you're forcing it, but because it feels good. You feel good.

That's the real shift.

And it starts with a glass, a pinch of salt, and your full attention.

GRATITUDE FIRST, GOALS SECOND

Most people wake up and instantly think about everything they haven't done yet. Their mind jumps straight into the logistics of the day: deadlines, errands, meetings, chores, messages. It's as if the brain opens with a browser tab full of urgency. But what if we changed the order? What if, instead of launching right into output mode, you began with a pause—a soft moment of gratitude—before moving into plans and productivity?

This idea isn't about ignoring your goals. It's about placing them second, not because they're unimportant, but because they land better when your mind isn't already tangled up in lack.

Gratitude first. Goals second. It's a rewire that shifts your whole relationship to effort and ambition.

Why Gratitude Before Goals Works

Think of your morning mind as soil. Gratitude enriches that soil, making it more receptive to the seeds you're about to plant—your intentions, your focus, your energy. Start your day in a state of thankfulness, and your goals grow from calm confidence instead of anxious striving.

There's a biochemical layer here too. Studies from institutions like the University of California, Davis, have shown that even short bursts of focused gratitude can increase dopamine and serotonin levels—your body's feel-good chemicals. And here's the kicker: these aren't just "happy" hormones. They also help with clarity, patience, and problem-solving. All of which you'll need once you shift into goal-setting mode.

On the flip side, starting your day with nothing but a to-do list can trigger your body's stress response. Elevated cortisol first thing in the morning doesn't just feel bad—it can throw off your digestion, mood, and decision-making for hours.

So, gratitude isn't some fluff. It's a neurological reset.

How to Start With Gratitude (Without Sounding Like a Self-Help Meme)

This doesn't have to be complicated. No need for a gratitude journal with gold-foiled pages or perfect calligraphy. It can be quiet, messy, even groggy. All that matters is the shift in attention. Try this:

- Right after your morning drink, before checking your phone, pause.
- Think of one thing you're grateful for—not five, not ten. One is enough.
- It doesn't have to be deep. Your dog snoring beside you. The way sunlight hits your floor. A friend who texted you back yesterday.
- Say it out loud if you can. If not, say it in your head like you mean it.

You're not trying to force joy. You're just noticing something already good. That's the key.

Then—and Only Then—Set a Goal

After you've anchored yourself in gratitude, now's the moment to think about your goals for the day. But here's where this method takes a turn: don't start with your biggest or hardest goal. Start with the one that aligns with how you want to feel.

That's different from productivity as most people approach it. This isn't about getting the most done—it's about getting the right things done from the right place.

Ask yourself: "What's one thing I could do today that would make me feel aligned, capable, or proud?"

That might be sending an email you've been avoiding. Or going for a walk after lunch. Or eating a real breakfast instead of skipping it again.

It's small—but it's yours. And because you led with gratitude, it's not loaded with pressure.

Real-Life Examples of This Switch

Let's talk about someone named Sofia. She's a busy mom, runs a freelance business, and barely gets ten quiet minutes a day. She used to wake up with her phone in hand, scanning emails and Instagram before she even sat up. Every morning felt frantic.

Then she made one small shift: no phone for the first five minutes. Instead, she sipped her pink salt drink and silently thought of one thing she appreciated. Sometimes it was just "I'm glad I have a dishwasher." Then she'd pick one meaningful task for the day—not ten. Just one.

She didn't suddenly become a productivity guru. But she noticed she was less reactive. She felt steadier. And strangely enough, she got more done.

That's the power of putting gratitude before goals. It sets a human tone to your morning.

The Neuroscience of Sequencing

The sequence here is everything. Gratitude triggers your parasympathetic nervous system—rest and restore. That means you're primed to make thoughtful decisions rather than reactive ones. Then, when you move into goal-setting, your brain isn't trying to multi-task between stress and strategy.

It's like warming up your car in winter. You don't floor the gas the second you turn the key. You let it hum for a minute. Then you drive.

Your mind works the same way. Gratitude is the ignition. Goals are the route.

This Isn't About Toxic Positivity

Let's be clear—this isn't about pretending everything is fine. Gratitude doesn't erase hardship. It just gives your mind something steady to hold onto while you move through it.

If you're in a hard season, your "one grateful thing" might feel small. That's okay. Gratitude is not a denial of pain—it's a quiet rebellion against it.

And when you follow it up with a clear, grounded goal, you're reclaiming agency over your day. Not just floating in reaction, but choosing action. With care.

Try This Tomorrow Morning

If you're curious to experiment with this practice, here's a lightweight version you can do in under five minutes:

- Drink your morning elixir slowly.
- Think of one thing you're grateful for. Just one.
- State it silently, or whisper it aloud.
- Then name one goal for the day—not your biggest task, but your clearest intention.
- Let both thoughts sit with you for a moment. That's it. Then move on with your day.

No apps needed. No notebooks. Just a new sequence that says: "First, I see what's good. Then, I decide what's next." That's a rhythm worth repeating.

GENTLE MOVEMENT (OPTIONAL BUT POWERFUL)

Movement doesn't have to be dramatic to be meaningful. In fact, the first five minutes of your day are arguably the worst time to sprint into a burpee routine or power through a heavy workout. Your body isn't there yet—and that's okay. Gentle movement is a way to whisper to your system: "Hey, we're awake. Let's warm up together." This isn't about burning calories. It's about connecting your breath, your body, and your mind right after rising.

Why Your Body Needs a Slow Start

When you wake up, your nervous system is shifting from rest mode into a more alert state. Blood pressure begins to rise, but your circulation is still sluggish. Your spine has been horizontal for hours, and your joints may feel stiff. In this state, aggressive activity can feel jarring—or even lead to injury.

Gentle movement offers a kind transition. You're not forcing your body to perform. You're inviting it to engage. Think of it like stretching a rubber band: pull too hard, too fast, and it snaps. But stretch slowly, and it becomes elastic again.

There's also the mental layer. Low-intensity movement first thing in the morning supports focus and calm. It helps you shake off grogginess and primes your brain for clarity—without overstimulating your system with stress hormones.

What Counts as Gentle Movement?

We're not talking about full yoga sessions or complex mobility routines (unless that's your thing). Gentle movement could be as simple as three to five minutes of intuitive motion that connects you with your breath.

Here are some ideas:

- Standing cat-cow rolls for your spine
- Slow neck and shoulder circles
- Forward folds with bent knees to wake up your hamstrings
- Side stretches with a big inhale to open your ribs
- Seated twists to get your digestive system going
- A few rounds of deep squats, moving with your breath

The goal is not precision—it's presence. You're waking up your tissues, not sculpting them.

From Stillness to Flow: A Sample Mini Sequence

If you're someone who likes structure, this three-minute sequence is a simple place to begin. No mat needed, no gear, no playlist.

1. **Neck Rolls** — Roll your head gently in circles, pausing anywhere that feels sticky. Breathe into it.
2. **Shoulder Rolls** — Bring your shoulders up to your ears, then roll them back and down. Repeat five times.
3. **Spinal Wave** — With soft knees, tuck your chin and roll down slowly. Let your arms dangle. Then roll back up one vertebra at a time.
4. **Side Stretch** — Reach your right arm overhead and lean gently to the left. Switch sides.
5. **Gentle Twist** — Standing or seated, twist from your waist to the right, then left. Don't force it—let it be light and fluid.

End by placing both hands over your belly and taking three deep breaths. That's it.

The Nervous System Response

Why does this matter? Because how you move first thing influences how your nervous system sets its tone for the rest of the day.

Gentle movement signals safety to your brain. When your body feels safe, you enter a parasympathetic state—sometimes called "rest and digest." This is the mode in which your body heals, focuses, and regulates appetite and hormones. Contrast that with jolting into the day through stress or tension, which activates fight-or-flight responses even when there's no actual danger.

So by moving slowly, intentionally, you're not just "warming up"—you're telling your brain and gut, "We're okay."

Who Benefits Most From This?

While everyone can gain something from this kind of movement, it's especially useful for:

- People with morning stiffness or chronic tension
- Anyone recovering from stress, burnout, or poor sleep
- Women navigating hormonal shifts, including perimenopause
- People with digestion issues or slow metabolism in the morning
- Those who want to feel more connected to their body, not fight it

Even high performers—entrepreneurs, athletes, parents—can benefit from starting their day with softness. It's a reset button that doesn't demand perfection.

Real-World Example: Movement as Morning Mindset

Consider Mark, a former competitive cyclist now working a high-stress tech job. He used to begin each day with a 6 a.m. power ride. It left him sweaty—but also anxious. He couldn't shake the feeling that he was sprinting through life, even before coffee.

After burning out, he replaced his morning routine with five minutes of slow joint mobility and deep breathing. At first, he felt guilty. Like it "wasn't enough." But after a few weeks, he noticed something strange: he didn't crash by 3 p.m. anymore. He was less reactive in meetings. And he still hit the gym later—only now with energy instead of adrenaline.

This is the quiet magic of gentle movement. It meets you where you are.

Optional—But Influential

Is this practice required? Of course not. That's the point. It's optional because you get to decide what your morning needs. But it's powerful because it creates space between waking up and rushing out.

If all you have is one minute, take one. If you've never stretched before, start with one move. Let it be small. Let it be yours. Because your body remembers how you treat it in the quiet moments before the day begins. And those moments? They shape everything that comes next.

TUNE IN, NOT SCROLL DOWN

Let's get honest: the first thing most people touch in the morning isn't their journal or a glass of lemon water—it's their phone. And not to check the weather or set an intention, but to swipe through an avalanche of updates, pings, photos, and noise. You may tell yourself it's just a quick peek, but that peek becomes ten minutes of someone else's life, opinions, or chaos entering yours before you've even said good morning to yourself. "Tuning in" instead of scrolling down isn't just a nice idea—it's a radical shift in how you choose to start your day.

The Moment Before the Momentum

You wake up. You breathe. You're still in that hazy state between sleep and wakefulness—what neuroscientists call the "theta window." In this state, your brain is more suggestible. Whatever you feed it in the first few minutes can color your thoughts, mood, and focus for hours.

So, when your hand reaches for your phone before your feet hit the ground, you're essentially letting the world jump into your nervous system before you've claimed it for yourself. You've started your day reacting, not choosing.

On the flip side, tuning in means asking one powerful question: "What do I need right now?" Not what your inbox needs. Not what the algorithm thinks you should want. Just you, breathing, present, awake to yourself.

Why This Shift Matters More Than Ever

Your attention is currency. And platforms know this. Apps are built to hook your brain with endless stimulation—likes, reels, red dots, DMs. The dopamine hits are real, but so is the cost. Morning screen time is linked to:

- Increased cortisol levels and anxiety
- Shorter attention spans throughout the day
- Disrupted natural circadian rhythms
- Reduced self-regulation and impulse control
- Greater comparison-based thinking (hello, social media)

But perhaps the biggest loss? The silence. The pause. That sacred moment where you meet your own thoughts before they're crowded out.

So What Does "Tuning In" Actually Look Like?

You don't have to meditate on a mountain or write six pages in your journal. Tuning in can be simple, accessible, even playful. It's anything that brings your attention back to your internal world—your breath, your sensations, your mindset.

Here are a few examples:

- Placing one hand on your heart and taking three slow breaths
- Repeating a grounding phrase like "I'm here, I'm awake, I'm enough"
- Stepping outside barefoot for 60 seconds to feel the ground
- Letting your mind wander with a cup of tea—no agenda, just noticing
- Writing down one feeling, one thought, and one intention

The common thread? You're the source of the input—not a glowing screen feeding you someone else's priorities.

Real Story: Breaking the Scroll Loop

Take Sophie, a freelance designer and self-described "doomscroll addict." She didn't start her days with creativity; she started with other people's lives. In her words, "By 8 a.m., I already felt behind."

One morning, she set her phone outside the bedroom. Instead of grabbing it, she placed her feet on the floor and said out loud, "What's mine today?" The first few mornings felt strange—quiet, even boring. But by the second week, she noticed her thoughts were clearer. She sketched more. She fought less with her partner. Her brain felt like it had space.

That's not magic. That's what reclaiming your attention does.

Still Want Your Phone in the Morning? Try This

Let's be realistic—not everyone wants to go full digital detox at dawn. If you still plan to use your phone early in the day, the key is how.

- Use it only for music or meditations (not apps that require scrolling)
- Turn on grayscale mode—less visual stimulation
- Disable notifications until a specific time of day
- Create a "morning screen" with just your weather, journal app, and timer
- Set a lockout on social media until after breakfast or movement

Tuning in doesn't mean becoming tech-averse. It means becoming tech-intentional.

Why This Helps Build Emotional Resilience

When you start your day by connecting inward instead of outward, you build what psychologists call internal locus of control. That's the belief that your mood, actions, and choices come from you—not what happens around you.

Over time, this builds resilience. You're less reactive to stress, more anchored during overwhelm, and more likely to move from purpose instead of pressure.

Morning tuning is one of the few practices that costs nothing, takes little time, and creates compounding returns. The hardest part? Remembering to pause.

But here's the good news: the first minute you choose yourself over your screen is already a win. You've chosen presence over pressure. And that choice? It ripples through everything that follows.

KEEP IT LIGHT, BUT CONSISTENT

Consistency. It's the word that shows up in every habit book, every podcast, every motivational quote slapped on a water bottle. But let's face it—it's also the word that can feel the heaviest. Why? Because when most people hear "consistency," they imagine perfection. No missed days. No excuses. No flexibility. That mindset can quickly lead to all-or-nothing thinking: either you're doing it perfectly every day, or you've failed. But that's not what true consistency looks like—especially in the context of a morning ritual designed to support your well-being, not stress you out.

When we say "keep it light, but consistent," we mean this: commit to showing up, but don't make the ritual feel like a chore. Make it so easy, so enjoyable, and so quick that skipping it feels more unnatural than doing it.

Why Lightness Matters

There's a reason diets and detoxes rarely last. They're built on the idea that effort equals effectiveness. But research—and lived experience—tells us that sustainability comes from ease. Your morning ritual should feel like a gift, not another item on a to-do list. If you dread it, you're not going to stick with it. And even if you do, you won't get the full mental and emotional benefit.

Keeping it light might mean:

- Choosing a three-minute version of your ritual instead of ten

- Sipping your pink salt water while stretching in bed
- Saying your intention for the day in the shower
- Listening to a calming song instead of journaling

The point isn't to dilute the power of the practice—it's to meet yourself where you are, especially on the mornings when life feels chaotic.

The Science Behind Repetition

In behavioral psychology, repetition is key to habit formation. But here's what most people miss: your brain doesn't need grand gestures to create a habit. It needs frequency. And it needs a clear trigger.

Let's break that down. Say you want to solidify your morning ritual. You pair it with something you already do every day—waking up, brushing your teeth, boiling water. That's your cue. Then you do the ritual, even if it's just one minute of stillness or sipping your salt water with awareness. That's your action. Over time, your brain starts to associate the cue with the behavior, and it becomes automatic.

You don't need 30 minutes of silence on a yoga mat. You need five consistent breaths every morning after you rinse your face. That's enough to rewire your brain's association with your morning.

Real-Life Example: Consistency That Works

James, a high-performing copywriter who described himself as "addicted to productivity," initially tried to turn his morning ritual into a full checklist: meditation, journaling, pink salt water, a gratitude log, ten push-ups. Unsurprisingly, he dropped it after four days.

What worked for him? Choosing one action—drinking his pink salt water—and linking it to one phrase he said out loud every morning: "I'm here, I'm ready, I've got this." It took less than a minute. But he did it for 30 days straight, even on vacation. That one moment became his anchor. From there, he naturally added more when he had time. But the foundation was built on ease, not effort.

When Consistency Meets Flexibility

Rigid routines break. Flexible ones bend. That's the philosophy behind this entire 5-minute morning ritual: it's about rhythm, not rules.

If you're traveling, if you're sick, if your toddler wakes up early—your ritual can still happen. Just shrink it. If your usual movement is a ten-minute stretch, make it three. If your typical gratitude practice is a journal entry, say it in your head instead.

The trick is to protect the *essence* of your ritual, not its exact format.

How to Stick with It (Even When You Don't Feel Like It)

Motivation is overrated. The people who stick with habits aren't more disciplined—they've just made it easier to follow through. Here's how:

- Place your pink salt water setup on your nightstand as a visual cue
- Use the same calming playlist each morning to create a mood shift
- Keep a sticky note with your ritual steps by your bathroom mirror
- Text a friend once a week sharing one thing your ritual helped you notice
- Track it with a simple checkbox calendar—not for guilt, just awareness

The moment you remove the pressure to "do it right," you create space to just do it.

The Compound Effect of Small Acts

One minute of tuning in every day is more powerful than an hour once a month. This is called the compound effect. Like compound interest, the results aren't dramatic at first—but they build. And suddenly, you realize you're calmer before meetings. You're less reactive to emails. You feel more grounded, more often.

The most interesting part? The lightness becomes the magnet. You look forward to the ritual. It feels like a return to self, not a departure from your time. It becomes something you crave—not out of discipline, but because it simply feels good.

And when something feels good, you'll keep coming back. That's the quiet power of consistency that doesn't demand perfection—it just asks for presence.

CHAPTER 8

Troubleshooting & Real-Life Adaptation

WHAT IF YOU MISS A DAY?

Let's start here: missing a day doesn't mean you've failed. It means you're human. And any habit that breaks the first time life gets unpredictable isn't one worth building in the first place. The real question isn't *"Did I skip a day?"* It's *"What happens next?"*

People often treat consistency like a tightrope walk—one wrong step and you're off the rope entirely. But in reality, forming habits is more like walking through a forest path. Some days you stride. Some days you stroll. Some days you sit down on a rock and just breathe. The path doesn't disappear because you stopped moving. It's still there, waiting.

Why We Fear "The Miss"

When someone misses a day in a new routine—whether it's a morning ritual, a new hydration habit, or a pink salt practice—the first response is often guilt. Guilt, followed by a story: "I'm just not disciplined enough." "This always happens." "I'll start over Monday." But these reactions aren't rooted in truth—they're rooted in perfectionism.

Perfectionism is sneaky. It hides behind your best intentions. It whispers that if you don't do something perfectly, it's not worth doing at all. That mindset kills more habits than laziness ever could.

Behavioral psychologist Dr. BJ Fogg explains that consistency builds through celebration, not shame. That means when you miss a day, the most productive thing you can do is... let it go. No mental spreadsheets. No self-punishment. Just return.

Re-entry Is the Real Skill

Let's talk about the muscle that actually sustains long-term habits: the skill of *re-entry*. It's not your ability to power through when life is smooth—it's your ability to bounce back when it's not. When your kids are sick. When your alarm fails. When you're traveling. When you're just exhausted.

You don't need to re-enter at full speed. You just need to show up again, even if it's clumsy. Even if it's late. Even if it looks different than usual.

Here's what that might look like:

- You forgot your pink salt drink? Just sip a tall glass of plain water and say your intention aloud. Done.
- You skipped your ritual entirely? No problem. Do a 10-second reset before lunch. That counts.
- You're feeling "off track"? That's a sign to scale back, not push harder. Make it easy again.

The re-entry mindset is what keeps people in motion without burning them out.

Real-Life Proof: Grace Over Grind

Carmen, a small business owner in her early 40s, started her pink salt ritual strong. But during the second week, her son caught a stomach bug, and her mornings turned into triage. She missed three days. Old her would've abandoned the routine entirely. This time, she reminded herself: missing a few days doesn't cancel the progress she made.

Instead of trying to "catch up," she just restarted the following morning with a 60-second version of her ritual. No guilt. No overthinking. Just water, breath, and presence. By week three, she was back to her full five-minute flow—stronger, actually, because she had proof that missing days didn't knock her off course. It made her more resilient.

Your Habit Is Not a Test

Many people subconsciously treat a new habit like it's pass/fail. Did you do it perfectly for 21 days? No? Then you failed. But habits aren't exams. They're tools. And tools are meant to serve *you*—not the other way around.

It helps to remember that your morning ritual isn't a contract. It's a conversation. And sometimes the answer that day is, "Not now." That's valid. But the conversation continues tomorrow.

Try This: A "Miss Day" Protocol

You don't need to overcorrect when you miss a day. But having a plan for how you respond can prevent the guilt spiral. Here's a simple one:

- Acknowledge it. "I didn't do my ritual this morning." That's all. Say it without judgment.
- Re-center with one breath or intention. One small anchor, even midday, brings you back.
- Commit to a 60-second version tomorrow. Just the salt drink. Just one stretch. Just the music.
- Mark your return. Circle it on a calendar or note it in your journal. Celebrate it mentally.

This isn't about discipline—it's about identity. Every time you return to your habit, even imperfectly, you reinforce, "I'm someone who shows up for myself."

When a Miss Becomes a Pattern

Okay, what if it's not just one day? What if it's been a week? A month?

That's not a failure either—but it *is* feedback.

If your ritual keeps falling through the cracks, it may be:

- Too long
- Too rigid
- Not connected to a trigger (like waking up or brushing teeth)
- Missing an emotional reward

Ask yourself: "What would make this feel easier to return to?" Sometimes the answer is simplifying. Sometimes it's making it more fun. Sometimes it's as simple as changing the time of day.

And sometimes, the best move is letting go of the structure entirely—and starting fresh with a new version that fits who you are *now*, not who you were when you started.

Consistency Isn't About Perfection—It's About Return

The beauty of this ritual is that it was never about strictness. It's about *relationship*. The relationship you build with yourself, one mindful sip at a time. That relationship will ebb and flow. And just like any relationship, what matters most isn't that it's always perfect. It's that you keep coming back.

DEALING WITH CRAVINGS AND PMS

Let's face it—cravings don't care about your wellness goals. They show up uninvited, often loud and persuasive, especially when hormones are shifting and your energy is uneven. Combine that with premenstrual symptoms, and it's not just a case of "I could really use a snack." It's more like "I need salt, sugar, carbs, now—or I might cry." Sound familiar?

What you're experiencing isn't weakness or lack of discipline. It's biology. And it can absolutely be worked with—not fought against.

Understanding the Root of Cravings

Cravings aren't random. They're signals. Sometimes, they're physical—your body asking for more calories, hydration, or micronutrients. Other times, they're emotional—comfort mechanisms triggered by stress, fatigue, or even boredom.

During PMS, cravings are particularly tied to hormonal fluctuations. Estrogen and progesterone dip, serotonin drops, and cortisol may rise. That combo leaves many women feeling moodier, hungrier, and more fatigued. So when your body says "Give me chocolate," it's not a lie. It's asking for a serotonin boost.

Add to that bloating, inflammation, and sluggish digestion, and it's easy to understand why staying "on plan" feels impossible. But here's the twist: the pink salt trick was actually built for moments like this.

Salt Cravings and Mineral Imbalance

One of the most common PMS cravings? Salt.

If you've ever found yourself demolishing a bag of chips or craving pickles out of nowhere, you're not alone. While some of that might be psychological, the root is often tied to fluctuating fluid levels. When estrogen rises before your period, it can lead to water retention—causing bloating and triggering the adrenal glands. Your body may respond by trying to self-regulate with salty foods.

Here's where pink salt comes in.

A small amount of pink salt in your water—especially when paired with lemon or a splash of apple cider vinegar—can help maintain electrolyte balance without the crash that comes from packaged snacks. It satisfies your salt craving, supports hydration, and reduces the urge to binge salty junk later.

One woman in her 30s shared that her pre-period craving for potato chips used to hit like clockwork. Once she started her pink salt water ritual daily (especially increasing intake a few days before her cycle began), the need to reach for processed salty foods dropped by more than half. The craving didn't disappear—but it got quieter, and more manageable.

Sugar, Serotonin, and That "Snacky" Feeling

Sugar cravings during PMS are legendary—and again, serotonin plays a starring role. When serotonin drops, the body starts seeking ways to stimulate it. Carbs—particularly fast-digesting ones—do exactly that. That's why sweets, bread, and pasta seem so much more appealing in the days before your period.

Now, cutting all sugar isn't necessary, and honestly, it's not helpful. Restriction often backfires. But pairing the right kind of carbs with fiber, protein, or healthy fat can give your brain what it's looking for without the crash that comes from a bag of cookies.

- Try this instead:
- A small bowl of Greek yogurt with berries and cinnamon
- A slice of sourdough toast with almond butter and a drizzle of raw honey
- Chia pudding made with coconut milk, topped with cacao nibs

These options satisfy that sweet craving while keeping your blood sugar steady. And yes, they *still feel like snacks.*

PMS and Emotional Triggers

Sometimes the craving isn't about food—it's about the need for comfort.

During PMS, sensitivity spikes. Things that normally roll off your back can feel sharp or overwhelming. Food becomes a way to soften the edge, to ground you, to soothe. And that's not wrong. It just means your nervous system is asking for something—safety, rhythm, familiarity.

That's why this chapter's earlier ritual practices can be a quiet but powerful ally. Starting your morning with intention (even a 3-minute breath, salt sip, and a song you love) sets the tone for the rest of the day. You're not just reacting—you're responding. That shift reduces the pull of emotional cravings later on.

Pink Salt as a PMS Support Tool

Here's where the pink salt ritual becomes more than just a hydration hack—it becomes cycle support.

If you're noticing a pattern in your cravings around your period, try adjusting your salt routine:

- Start increasing your pink salt water 3–5 days before your expected period
- Add magnesium-rich foods during that time (like pumpkin seeds, dark leafy greens, or even a magnesium supplement if needed)
- Stay hydrated but not overhydrated—too much water without minerals can increase bloating, not reduce it

Many women report that the combination of hydration, minerals, and predictable routine helps stabilize mood swings and decreases the spike in cravings that used to feel overwhelming.

Real-Life Tip: Build an "Emergency Craving Plan"

Because let's be honest—some days, all the rituals in the world won't stop the craving train. That's okay. But instead of relying on willpower alone, create a system that helps you pivot.

- Set up a mini "PMS drawer" in your kitchen. It can include:
- Dark chocolate squares (ideally 70% or higher)
- Pink salt cashews or tamari almonds
- A quality herbal tea blend for mood and bloating (like raspberry leaf or peppermint)
- One or two grab-and-go snack packs you actually enjoy, not just tolerate

This isn't about eliminating cravings—it's about handling them with kindness and awareness.

Cravings as a Check-In, Not a Crisis

Here's the takeaway: cravings don't make you broken. They make you *responsive.* Your body is talking to you. The trick isn't to silence it—it's to listen better.

So next time that wave of craving hits—salty, sweet, or carb-loaded—pause. Ask what your body actually wants. And remember, pink salt isn't just a trick. It's a signal to slow down, check in, and respond with care.

HOW TO TRAVEL WITH THE TRICK

Travel has a unique ability to throw even the best intentions out the window. Whether you're heading to a work conference, a beach getaway, or a family reunion, routines tend to go blurry the moment you zip up a suitcase. The pink salt trick—simple as it is—can be one of the easiest parts of your wellness habits to take with you. But only if you plan for it.

Why Travel Disrupts the Body More Than We Think

Let's start by acknowledging what happens to your body when you're on the move. Travel can dehydrate you (hello, dry airplane air), mess with your digestion (airport food isn't exactly light and fibrous), and disrupt your sleep and circadian rhythm—especially if you're crossing time zones.

Combine all that with long hours sitting still, unexpected stress, and less control over meals, and your body starts to feel like it's running on fumes. That's where the pink salt ritual becomes less of a luxury and more of a lifeline.

The small shot of minerals from quality pink salt helps support hydration, adrenal balance, and cellular function—all of which are taxed during travel. It's not about perfection. It's about giving your body something reliable, grounding, and easy to maintain.

Pre-Trip Planning: Build a "Travel-Size Ritual Kit"

The biggest barrier to keeping a wellness habit alive on the road isn't willpower—it's logistics. So let's make this brainless.

Create a grab-and-go kit that includes:
- A small travel container of pink Himalayan salt (a 2 oz spice jar works perfectly)
- Portable bottle of lemon juice or a few lemon packets
- A collapsible water bottle or your favorite sturdy reusable one
- Travel-friendly electrolyte powder (unsweetened if possible) as a backup for longer trips or hot destinations

Toss this into your carry-on or purse, and you're always one step ahead of dehydration. And the best part? Unlike supplements or liquids, dry salt rarely gets flagged by airport security.

In-Transit Strategies: Stay Ahead of Dehydration

Flights are notorious for dehydrating the body. The low cabin humidity can cause your cells to lose water faster than usual—even if you don't feel thirsty. Add in coffee or in-flight alcohol, and your electrolyte balance can tank quickly.

Before boarding, sip a bottle of water mixed with a pinch of pink salt and a squeeze of lemon. This primes your system before the dry air sets in. During the flight, avoid overdoing caffeine and try to sip consistently, not just chug when you remember.

Driving instead? The same rules apply. Keep your water bottle within reach, and refill it at every stop with a quick shake of salt. It's not glamorous, but your energy and digestion will thank you later.

Hotel Habits: Keep It Simple and Predictable

One of the biggest traps of travel is inconsistency. You wake up in a strange room, eat at odd hours, and sometimes forget what day it is. Anchoring yourself with a ritual—something that feels familiar—can bring calm and clarity.

Make your pink salt water your "travel toothbrush." In other words, treat it like something you do *before* everything else. When you wake up, grab your water bottle, add salt and lemon, and drink before checking your phone, getting dressed, or heading to breakfast.

Even if you've had a late night, a long meeting, or a change in schedule, that tiny moment reminds your body: *We're still taking care of you.*

If you're in a hotel with a mini fridge, you can even prep a second bottle for the next day—no excuses required.

Eating Out and Staying Balanced

Restaurant food and travel snacks can be high in sodium but low in actual minerals. It's a strange irony—your body feels bloated and depleted at the same time.

That's why using real salt intentionally is such a helpful contrast. By starting your day with pink salt, you give your body the minerals it actually wants, which can cut down on cravings for ultra-processed foods later on.

Another travel trick: order a sparkling water with lemon at restaurants. Not only does it support digestion, but if you carry your own small salt jar (yes, seriously), you can add a pinch to your drink discreetly. It's your ritual—own it.

When You Forget or Miss a Day

Here's the thing: even with the best planning, you might skip your pink salt water one morning. Or two. Maybe you're running late, you forgot your kit, or you're just out of rhythm. That's normal. The key is not to throw in the towel.

Habits don't break from one skipped day—they break when guilt sets in and convinces you it's not worth restarting.

Instead, view each morning as a clean slate. Your pink salt water is just waiting to pick up where you left off. Whether it's day 2 or day 200, the ritual still works.

Real Life Story: The "Airport Ritual"

One woman who started the 21-day plan shared a story that speaks to the power of this habit. She had a red-eye flight from New York to L.A., got almost no sleep, and landed cranky and bloated. Normally, that would've meant a muffin and a triple latte to "reset." But she had her little travel salt kit. She mixed it with a bottle of water while waiting for her ride, sipped it slowly, and felt a noticeable difference in 15 minutes. "It didn't fix everything," she said, "but it stopped me from crashing. I felt more like myself."

That's the point. Travel doesn't have to derail your routine. With one small, thoughtful ritual, you give your body a sense of stability in the middle of chaos. And that might be more powerful than anything you packed.

ADJUSTING FOR COLD WEATHER, WORK LIFE, OR FAMILY ROUTINE

Let's be honest—life rarely rolls out the red carpet for our habits. Just when you're getting into a groove with the pink salt trick, life throws you a seasonal shift, an office deadline, or a kid with the flu. That's not failure. That's real life. The good news? This trick isn't about rigidity—it's about adaptability.

Cold Weather Challenges: Why Your Body Reacts Differently

Winter changes everything. Your hydration needs, energy patterns, even your cravings. And that affects how your body responds to the pink salt ritual. Cold air tends to dry out your respiratory tract, even if you don't feel as thirsty. Heating systems indoors do the same. You sweat less, but you still lose fluids through breath and urination—so the hydration support you get from pink salt becomes even more relevant.

But there's another layer: digestion often slows in colder months. Your body naturally craves heavier meals and warm comfort foods. That's not bad, but it can make your usual morning routine feel "off." If cold water with lemon and salt doesn't appeal first thing in the morning, there's an easy fix—make it warm.

Try a mug of warm water with a pinch of pink salt and a squeeze of lemon. It still provides the minerals and hydration, but with a cozier feel. You can even steep ginger slices for digestion or a cinnamon stick if your appetite's gone rogue.

This isn't about changing the habit—it's about letting it evolve with the season.

Morning Mayhem: Work Schedules That Leave No Room

Some people wake up to sunlight and birdsong. Others wake up to email pings and screaming toddlers. If you're in the second group, squeezing in a health ritual may feel laughable.

But remember: the pink salt trick takes less than a minute. It doesn't need perfect silence or a yoga mat. What it *does* need is predictability.

If your mornings are chaotic, build the ritual into a non-negotiable part of your routine. For example:

- Keep your water bottle by your toothbrush and take your salt-lemon shot right after brushing.
- If you rely on coffee to wake up, make the salt drink the "cover charge" before the coffee.
- Pre-mix your water bottle the night before and store it in the fridge for grab-and-go ease.

Think of it as the thing you do *before* the rest of the day tries to take over. A tiny moment of control before the emails and school drop-offs start piling up.

Working from Home vs. Office Dynamics

Remote work sounds like it should make routines easier, right? You have more time, more flexibility… and also more distractions. The kitchen is ten feet away, your phone is always nearby, and that "just five more minutes" delay can turn into skipping your ritual entirely.

Set a recurring reminder on your phone—ideally at the same time you boot up your computer. Or tie the ritual to an existing action, like starting your calendar for the day. Anchoring it to a task already in your work rhythm can keep it from falling through the cracks.

If you work in an office, the key is portability. Keep a small container of pink salt at your desk or in your bag. And if you're not keen on explaining your "weird pink salt water" to curious coworkers, pour it into a travel mug or thermos. No one needs to know what's in it. It's your habit—private, powerful, and portable.

Family Life: Building Habits That Work in Shared Spaces

Shared homes mean shared routines, and sometimes those routines conflict. If you live with a partner, kids, or roommates, carving out space for your own rituals can feel selfish. But it's not.

In fact, modeling small, grounded habits can be contagious in the best way. You may not convince your partner to drink salt water, but they might start rethinking their own hydration. Kids might ask what you're doing—and next thing you know, they're asking for lemon water too.

Still, mornings in a family household are rarely quiet. So streamline:

- Keep your ritual gear in one easy-access spot—lemon, salt, glass or bottle, done.
- If you pack school lunches or prep breakfast, keep your water close and sip while you prep.
- Let the pink salt water be part of "mom or dad time"—something quick that shows your own care matters, too.

You're not adding something to your list. You're protecting a habit that supports everything else on that list.

When Things Still Don't Go to Plan

There will be mornings when the baby won't stop crying. Or you sleep through your alarm. Or you're halfway to work before you remember the salt. That's not a crisis. It's just a skipped beat. You can always come back.

Some people switch the ritual to mid-morning or lunchtime when needed. That's fine. The impact is strongest when done early, but the habit's real power is consistency over time—not the exact hour it happens.

And in the colder months or during high-stress seasons, don't be surprised if your body *wants* the routine more. It may become a grounding force that offers calm when the rest of your life doesn't.

So adjust. Tweak. Pivot. But don't abandon the ritual. It's designed to bend with you. Whether it's winter windchill, Zoom meetings, or spilled cereal—it still fits.

CHAPTER 9
Smart Tools to Support Your Routine

PINK SALT RITUAL PREP CHECKLIST

Let's be honest—there's a difference between wanting to start a wellness habit and actually doing it every day. The gap between those two isn't willpower. It's preparation. A few simple setups the night before can make the difference between "I forgot" and "I crushed it before breakfast."

This isn't a one-size-fits-all kind of checklist. It's a flexible prep guide to help you build a system around your pink salt ritual, so it becomes as automatic as brushing your teeth. You don't need to be perfect—just prepared.

Why Prepping Matters More Than Motivation

You've probably experienced it before: you're excited to try something new, your energy is high, and you nail it the first two or three days. But then real life kicks in. You're running late, the kitchen is a mess, the lemons are moldy, and your salt jar is nowhere to be found.

Preparation removes decision fatigue. When everything you need is right in front of you, you don't have to think. You just do. That's what turns a habit into a lifestyle. It's not about willpower—it's about creating fewer obstacles between you and the habit.

The Night-Before Setup Strategy

The easiest way to stay consistent is to set the stage the night before. Think of it as laying out your clothes for the gym—except this time it's a lemon, a glass, and a pinch of pink salt.

Here's how to make it foolproof:

- Keep your salt in a visible, easy-to-reach spot—think countertop, not back of the pantry.
- Pre-slice a lemon or keep one on the counter as a visual cue.
- Use a small prep tray or dish to keep your ritual items together: your salt jar, a spoon, a lemon wedge, and your morning glass.
- If you use filtered or mineral water, fill your glass or bottle before bed and leave it on the counter or in the fridge.
- Set an optional reminder on your phone or smart speaker—"Drink your morning salt water."

This five-minute prep creates a chain reaction the next day. You see the setup, and your brain clicks into ritual mode without friction.

Make It Mobile: Travel and On-the-Go Prep

Some days aren't spent at home. You might have an early meeting or a flight to catch. That doesn't mean your ritual has to disappear. You just need a travel version of your setup.

A mobile kit can be a game changer. It doesn't need to be fancy. Toss the basics into a pouch, and you're ready for anything.

Travel kit ideas:

- Mini jar or zip pouch of pink salt
- Small bottle of lemon juice (the glass kind from organic brands lasts longer)
- Collapsible silicone cup or leak-proof water bottle
- Resealable bag for sliced lemon wedges (wrapped in parchment or beeswax paper)

Keep the pouch in your work bag, gym tote, or carry-on luggage. Now there's no excuse, even on the busiest mornings or when you're halfway across the country.

Don't Overcomplicate the Gear

There's a temptation to buy everything: the best salt grinder, the artisanal citrus press, fancy glass bottles. But the truth is, the pink salt ritual doesn't need gear to work. What matters most is consistency, not aesthetics.

Still, if having nice tools motivates you, here's what actually helps:

- Small ceramic or glass container for salt (easy access, looks good on the counter)
- Manual citrus squeezer (especially if arthritis or grip fatigue is a factor)
- Wide-mouth mason jars or glass water bottles with measurements (for batch prepping)
- Reusable metal or silicone straws if citrus water hurts your enamel

Let tools support your routine—but don't let them delay it. If all you have is a spoon, a lemon, and a mug, you're ready.

Batch-Prepping: Yes or No?

Some people like to make one glass each morning, fresh and warm. Others find it easier to mix two or three day's worth ahead of time and store it in the fridge.

Here's what works for each approach:

Fresh prep:

- Feels more mindful, especially when part of a morning ritual
- Encourages you to tune into how your body feels that day
- Good if you like your water warm

Batch prep:

- Perfect for hectic mornings or if you leave early
- Lets you grab and sip during your commute
- Useful if you're prepping for multiple people (family, roommates, etc.)

There's no right or wrong way here. Try both, see what feels easiest, and stick with it.

Keeping It Visible

If your ritual lives in the back of a cabinet or inside a drawer, it's already half-forgotten. Visibility is part of success.

Place your prep zone somewhere you naturally pass through in the morning—near the coffee machine, next to the sink, by the fridge handle. Let it become part of your visual landscape.

Some people even add a sticky note on the bathroom mirror: "Water + salt first." It sounds silly, but those gentle nudges can be the bridge between good intention and action.

Your Checklist: The Visual Reminder

You don't need to memorize anything. Just glance at this each night or tape it inside a cabinet:

- Is my salt jar easy to reach?
- Do I have a lemon (or lemon juice) ready?
- Is my glass or bottle out where I'll see it?
- Did I prep water (if I want it chilled or filtered)?
- Do I need my travel version for tomorrow?

One minute of prep can buy you an entire day of momentum. It's not just a drink—it's the spark for everything that comes after it.

"SWAP THIS FOR THAT" CLEAN SALT CHART

It's easy to fall into the trap of thinking all salt is created equal. After all, it's just salt, right? Not exactly. Depending on the source, processing method, and additives, the salt you're using could be quietly undermining your wellness goals—even if you're careful with everything else you eat and drink.

This section isn't about fearmongering. It's about practical swaps. A clean salt routine doesn't mean throwing everything in your pantry out—it means knowing what to look for, what to avoid, and how to make upgrades without overhauling your lifestyle.

Why Salt Quality Matters More Than You Think

Most people think about salt in terms of blood pressure, bloating, or taste. But when you're using salt as part of a functional wellness practice—like the pink salt morning ritual—its source and composition suddenly matter a lot more.

Heavily processed table salts are often stripped of natural minerals and then "enriched" with synthetic additives. These might include anti-caking agents, flow enhancers, and artificial iodine—none of which support the body's natural systems the way unrefined mineral salts can.

Think of it this way: you wouldn't expect the same nutrition from a fast-food burger and a grass-fed steak. So why would you expect the same benefits from highly bleached table salt and raw, mineral-rich pink salt?

The Table Salt Trap

Refined white salt (the kind in most salt shakers) might be convenient, but it comes with a few hidden downsides:

- Typically bleached to appear bright white
- Often contains aluminum-based anti-caking agents
- May include synthetic iodine, which isn't always well absorbed
- Lacks the natural trace minerals found in raw salts
- Can taste sharp or metallic compared to natural salts

If you're using it in large amounts—or as part of a daily ritual—you're essentially starting your day with something that's been through more processing than most people realize.

Enter Mineral-Rich Alternatives

Natural salts, like Himalayan pink salt or Celtic sea salt, aren't just about aesthetics. They provide over 80 trace minerals that support hydration, cellular function, and even nerve conduction. When you consume a small amount of mineral salt in the morning with water, you're not just replenishing sodium—you're offering your body a subtle nutrient signal that supports balance.

What makes these salts different?

- They're harvested with minimal processing (usually sun-dried)
- No anti-caking agents or bleaching chemicals
- Contain naturally occurring iodine—not synthetic forms
- Offer a milder, rounder flavor profile
- Color variations (pink, gray, beige) indicate mineral variety, not contamination

In short: they're salt the way nature intended.

Swap Chart: Common Salts and Their Better Counterparts

This chart isn't meant to shame your spice rack—it's a simple reference for when you're ready to upgrade, one pinch at a time.

IF YOU USE THIS…	TRY SWAPPING WITH THIS INSTEAD	WHY IT'S A BETTER FIT FOR THE RITUAL
Iodized table salt (white, fine)	Himalayan pink salt (fine grain)	Mineral-rich, unprocessed, clean flavor
Kosher salt (standard brand)	Celtic sea salt (light gray, moist)	Retains moisture and trace minerals
Rock salt (generic)	Redmond Real Salt (Utah-based)	Ancient salt bed, no additives, US origin
Sea salt (white, refined)	Hawaiian black salt (volcanic trace minerals)	Unique minerals and a deeper flavor
"Lite" salt (sodium-reduced)	Himalayan pink + potassium chloride (natural blend)	Keeps balance without synthetic cuts

Keep in mind: you don't need 12 different salts in your kitchen. One high-quality mineral salt can be your go-to for everything—from your morning ritual to cooking dinner.

Reading the Label Like a Pro

Labels can be misleading. If it says "sea salt" but it's snow-white and pours like powdered sugar, it's probably been processed.

Here's what to look for:

- Color that isn't bright white (pink, beige, gray = trace minerals)
- "Unrefined" or "raw" listed on the label
- No mention of anti-caking agents or additives
- Country or source of origin (e.g., Himalayas, France, Utah)
- Crystals that are irregular, slightly moist, or clumpy (a good sign!)

If you're unsure, smaller specialty brands tend to be more transparent than generic supermarket labels.

When Organic Doesn't Apply

Unlike produce, salt can't be certified organic. It doesn't grow in soil or require pesticides. So if you see a salt claiming "organic," that's a red flag—either it's misusing the term or using it for marketing.

Instead, look for origin traceability and clean sourcing methods. A salt harvested from a known, pollution-free source and dried without heat or chemicals is the gold standard.

Storing Your Salt the Right Way

You don't need fancy salt cellars or bamboo boxes (unless that brings you joy). But there are a few smart habits that preserve quality:

- Store in glass, ceramic, or stainless steel—not plastic
- Avoid exposing to moisture or steam (keep away from the stove)
- Use dry spoons to scoop—don't dip in with wet fingers
- Keep your ritual salt separate from your cooking salt if you prefer finer grains

These small steps keep the minerals intact and the flavor clean.

Final Thoughts Without the Summary

Every pinch matters—especially when it's part of your first action of the day. When you start with the right salt, you're not just sipping water. You're signaling to your body that quality matters, even in the smallest choices.

Let the clean salt swap be one of those quiet upgrades that makes your whole wellness rhythm feel more grounded. It's not about being perfect. It's about being aware—and ready.

"SALT + GLOW" SELF-CARE WEEKLY GUIDE

Wellness isn't something you do once and cross off a list. It's something you live—small choices, built on each other, that slowly shape how you feel in your body and show up in your life. That's the spirit behind the "Salt + Glow" guide. It's not a strict routine, not a rulebook. It's a rhythm. A loose, weekly pattern to help you weave your pink salt ritual into a deeper, more nourishing self-care flow.

Each day comes with a focus—one small area to tend to. You can follow it to the letter or use it as inspiration. The point isn't perfection. It's showing up, consistently and lightly, so you stay connected to your body instead of just managing it.

Monday: Ground and Hydrate

Mondays don't have to be manic. Start the week by getting back into your body and recharging from the inside out.

- Do your pink salt ritual slowly and intentionally—sit down, breathe, sip without multitasking.
- Drink water steadily throughout the day, not just in the morning. Add cucumber or mint for extra refreshment.
- Eat something grounding—like roasted root veggies or a warm grain bowl—for lunch or dinner.
- Take five minutes to stretch your lower body: feet, ankles, hamstrings. Grounding starts there.

This sets a tone of calm authority over your own time, instead of jumping straight into the whirlwind.

Tuesday: Clean Your Space, Clear Your Mind

Tidy space, tidy thoughts. Even a small reset in your surroundings can ripple into your mood and focus.

- Use a natural salt scrub (store-bought or DIY with pink salt and coconut oil) during your shower.
- Wipe down your kitchen counter or bathroom shelf where your morning ritual lives—make it shine.
- Declutter one drawer or shelf. Just one. The goal is to create flow, not stress yourself out.
- Light a candle or play calming music while you do it. Turn it into a mini ritual.

Your salt routine isn't just about what you consume—it's about the environment that supports it.

Wednesday: Move and Circulate

The middle of the week can feel sluggish. Get things flowing with gentle movement that boosts circulation.

- Do your pink salt water, then go for a brisk walk—even just around the block.
- Try dry brushing before your shower to stimulate the lymphatic system.
- Make a citrus-based smoothie (lemon, orange, ginger, salt) to refresh and awaken your senses.
- Stretch your arms and chest—areas that tighten from too much screen time.

Think of movement not as punishment, but as energy release. A way to shake off buildup—physically and mentally.

Thursday: Soothe and Support

This is your "check-in" day. How's your energy? Digestion? Mood? Adjust accordingly.

- Use your salt ritual to assess how you feel. Need more hydration? More rest?
- Try a mineral soak or foot bath with Epsom salt and pink salt together. Bonus if you add lavender.
- Make dinner feel like a ritual—set the table, slow down, put your phone away.
- If you're bloated or off, skip raw veggies and focus on warm, easy-to-digest foods tonight.

The goal isn't to fix anything—it's to listen and respond with care.

Friday: Glow from the Inside Out

You're almost at the weekend. Time to lean into beauty and confidence—but from the inside.

- Add turmeric or cayenne to your morning salt drink for a circulation kick (only if it suits your body).
- Use a face mask with clay or sea minerals—your skin reflects how your body feels inside.
- Write down three things that made you feel strong this week, even small ones.
- Do one "glam" thing that's just for you—lip color, earrings, outfit you love.

Glowing isn't about chasing trends. It's about recognizing your own vitality—and honoring it.

Saturday: Expand and Explore

The weekend invites space. Try something new, break your routine, or share your ritual with someone else.

- Bring your salt prep on a walk or picnic. Sip it outside if the weather's nice.
- Teach a friend or partner how to do the ritual, even if just for fun.

- Try a new fruit or herb in your salt water—pineapple, basil, rosemary, or grapefruit.
- Journal about how your body feels after a week of small daily rituals. What's shifted?

Rituals don't have to be private. Sharing them can make them even more powerful.

Sunday: Reflect and Reset

Before the new week starts, slow down. Reflect, prep, and reset your foundation.

- Batch prep lemon slices or water jars for the next three mornings.
- Refill your salt jar if it's low. Clean your ritual items if needed.
- Write a short intention for the coming week. Keep it simple and physical (e.g., "more stretching" or "better sleep").
- Do a "gratitude sip"—drink your water slowly, thinking of three things that went right this week.

This isn't about productivity. It's about finishing the week with clarity and starting the next with care.

Making the Weekly Flow Work for You

This guide isn't carved in stone. If Thursday ends up being your busiest day, maybe that's the day you focus on batch prepping instead of soaking. If you miss a day, no problem. You're not starting over—you're simply returning.

The beauty of this rhythm is that it evolves with you. Over time, it becomes second nature—not because you memorized it, but because your body remembers how good it feels when you show up for it, little by little.

So pick up your salt, sip with purpose, and let the rest follow. You've got the glow—you're just learning how to keep it lit.

CHAPTER 10
Going Beyond Weight Loss

HOW TO SHIFT FROM QUICK FIXES TO LONG-TERM GLOW

Most people don't fail at wellness because they're lazy or undisciplined. They struggle because they're stuck in a cycle of extremes: all-in, then all-out. And who can blame them? We live in a world that markets urgency as self-care. "Drop ten pounds in a week," "detox your body in three days," "skip breakfast and fix your metabolism." Sound familiar?

But what if your wellness didn't depend on a breakthrough product or a 30-day overhaul? What if it was more like brushing your teeth—consistent, almost automatic, and, honestly, kind of boring in the best way?

This is where glow replaces grind. Where maintenance beats momentum. Where your body stops being a project and starts being a partner.

Why Quick Fixes Work—Until They Don't

Quick fixes appeal to us for a reason: they feel like control. They offer immediate action and results. If you've been feeling bloated, sluggish, or frustrated, a plan that promises visible changes in days can feel like a lifeline.

But the flip side is that quick fixes don't teach you how to live—they just teach you how to comply. Once the structure is gone, you're back to square one. Worse, they often disconnect you from your own signals. You stop asking, "How do I feel?" and start asking, "What am I allowed to eat today?"

Quick fixes also train you to see progress as something you chase, not something you sustain. This sets up a fragile dynamic—if you're not "on track," you're off it. And that pressure is exhausting.

What Long-Term Glow Actually Looks Like

Glow, in this context, isn't about makeup or filters. It's a kind of energy. A sense of lightness in your skin, clarity in your thoughts, and steadiness in your habits. It's not flashy. It doesn't come with a dramatic before-and-after photo. But it shows up in small ways:

- You wake up thirsty instead of groggy.
- You get hungry at consistent times because your hormones are more stable.
- Your skin looks more even without having changed your skincare routine.
- You stop thinking about food as a problem to solve and start seeing it as support.

These changes are subtle but powerful. They're the kind of shifts that build on each other over time. The best part? You don't need to overhaul your life to start. You just need to stop treating your body like a short-term puzzle.

Building the Foundations of Longevity

Let's break this down into what actually creates that lasting glow—beyond trends, detoxes, or calorie counts.

1. Rhythm Over Rules

Instead of focusing on strict guidelines, aim to develop patterns. This means eating at roughly the same times each day. Sleeping and waking around the same hour. Drinking water when your body is naturally most dehydrated (morning, early afternoon).

It's not about never skipping a day—it's about having a rhythm that you return to easily.

2. Recovery as a Ritual

Long-term glow comes from how you bounce back, not how perfectly you stick to the plan. If you miss a week of pink salt rituals, you're not off the rails. You just pick it up again the next morning.

Recovery isn't an apology—it's a recalibration. You don't need guilt to resume.

3. Support Instead of Stress

The minute wellness becomes a source of stress, it's no longer serving its purpose. Your rituals should feel like scaffolding, not a straitjacket.

That means choosing things that are simple to repeat. Morning pink salt water? Two minutes. Taking a few breaths before eating? Zero cost. Consistency doesn't require complexity.

4. Identity Over Outcome

Here's where things get real. People who stick with long-term wellness often do it not because they're chasing a goal—but because it's just who they are now.

They don't say, "I'm trying to hydrate more." They say, "I drink water first thing every morning."

They don't say, "I'm on a new routine." They say, "This is how I start my day."

You shift your self-perception. And when that clicks, habits become expressions—not obligations.

Real Examples: What the Shift Looks Like in Practice

Let's talk through how this shift plays out in the real world.

- **Old Pattern:** You go all-in on a cleanse, drop five pounds, then binge on the weekend.
- **Glow Shift:** You start every day with salt water and notice your cravings drop by Friday.
- **Old Pattern:** You beat yourself up for skipping your morning walk.
- **Glow Shift:** You stretch for five minutes while your coffee brews instead.
- **Old Pattern:** You try a 12-hour fast because you saw it online, but it leaves you shaky.
- **Glow Shift:** You eat a mineral-rich breakfast when you feel tired and realize you needed fuel, not discipline.

This kind of adaptation builds trust in yourself. You're not following someone else's program. You're tuning into your own body and adjusting as needed.

Letting Go of Urgency

If there's one thing that will hold you back from long-term glow, it's the need to rush. Glow doesn't shout—it simmers. It builds quietly, beneath the surface, until one day you notice: your pants fit better, your face looks brighter, your mind feels clearer.

And no, there won't be a dramatic finish line. There will just be more days that feel a little easier. That's the point. You don't need a new start. You just need to keep going—one quiet, glowing step at a time.

BUILDING A WELLNESS IDENTITY, NOT JUST A GOAL

Ask someone why they're starting a wellness routine and the answers often come in numbers: pounds lost, inches off the waist, days on a detox. These are goals—short-term, measurable, often motivating. But what happens when the goal is reached? Or missed? That's where many people fall off the path—not because they lack discipline, but because they were chasing a finish line instead of building a foundation.

Goals aren't bad. They're just not enough. Real change doesn't come from hitting a number—it comes from becoming the kind of person who lives differently, even when no one's watching. That's the heart of a wellness identity.

From Doing to Being: The Identity Shift

There's a big difference between saying "I'm trying to eat healthier" and saying "I'm someone who eats to feel good." One is a task. The other is a trait. And when you start to see your wellness habits as part of who you are—not just what you do—you don't need as much motivation to keep going.

Behavioral psychology backs this up. Research shows that habits are more likely to stick when they're tied to identity. If you believe you're a runner, you're more likely to go for a jog, even when it's cold out. If you see yourself as someone who takes care of their body, you'll make choices in line with that belief—even if you're not trying to reach a goal right now.

This kind of internal shift is what separates a temporary wellness kick from a lifestyle you actually keep.

Identity Anchors: Tiny Actions That Build a Bigger Picture

So how do you build a wellness identity without getting stuck in perfectionism or burnout? It starts with small, repeated choices—identity anchors. These are the consistent actions that reinforce your self-image, day after day.

Examples of identity anchors:

- Drinking your pink salt water first thing, even on busy mornings
- Keeping a bottle of water on your desk as a cue to hydrate
- Choosing a mineral-rich snack over processed options—not because you "have to," but because it feels good
- Putting on your walking shoes, even if you only have time for a few minutes outside
- Listening to your body's signals and eating when you're truly hungry, not when the clock says it's time

These habits don't need to be dramatic. They just need to be yours. When you repeat them regularly, your brain begins to register: "This is who I am now." And that quiet confidence carries you farther than willpower ever could.

Letting Go of the Old Story

Often, people get stuck because they're clinging to old narratives: "I've always been inconsistent." "I fall off track every time I try." "I'll never be one of those healthy people."

Here's a mindset shift worth trying: Instead of asking if you're disciplined enough, ask whether the story you're telling yourself is still serving you. Because identity isn't fixed. It's fluid. And you're allowed to outgrow your past.

Try writing a new story that starts now—not someday when you've "earned it," but today, with the small choices already in your control.

Examples of identity-based statements:
- "I prioritize how I feel, not just how I look."
- "I hydrate because clarity matters to me."
- "I don't need a perfect routine—just one that supports me."
- "I trust myself to keep showing up."

These mantras aren't fluff—they're reframes. And repeating them helps replace outdated beliefs with something more grounded and helpful.

Flexibility: The Hallmark of a Real Identity

Let's be clear: building a wellness identity doesn't mean locking yourself into a rigid image. It means knowing who you are even when life throws a curveball. Flexibility is a feature, not a flaw.

Someone with a strong wellness identity doesn't crumble when the schedule shifts—they adapt. If their morning routine is interrupted, they might hydrate mid-morning instead. If they skip a planned workout, they stretch before bed.

This isn't failure. It's resilience. A wellness identity is built on consistency, not rigidity. You show up most days, in most situations. And when you don't, you don't spiral—you recalibrate.

Real-World Examples: From Concept to Lifestyle

Let's look at a few snapshots of what this identity shift can look like in practice.

Case 1: Vanessa, 39, entrepreneur.

Used to: Skip meals, crash diet twice a year.

Now: Keeps a morning mineral water ritual to feel grounded before meetings.

Identity anchor: "I'm a person who fuels my body like it's my business partner."

Case 2: Lara, 28, new mom.

Used to: Follow intense fitness plans, then burn out.

Now: Takes short walks daily and listens to an audiobook for mental reset.

Identity anchor: "I take care of myself so I can care for others."

Case 3: Mel, 46, teacher.

Used to: View wellness as a summer-only project.

Now: Uses the same 10-minute morning routine every school day, even if tired.

Identity anchor: "I start my day on my terms."

These aren't transformations that come with flashy headlines. But they're the kind that last—because they're grounded in how these people see themselves, not in chasing a result.

FINAL WORDS: YOU ARE NOT STARTING OVER—YOU'RE EVOLVING

Let's stop pretending that falling off a routine means failure. If you've ever told yourself, "I have to start all over again," you're not alone. That sentence gets whispered in gyms, kitchens, therapy rooms, and grocery aisles all over the world. But here's the thing: starting over isn't real. You are never actually back at square one.

You've already done the hardest part—you began. You tried something. You showed up for yourself, even inconsistently. That alone changes the equation. The next time you come back, you're doing it with more information, more self-awareness, and often, more clarity. That's not starting over. That's evolving.

The Illusion of the "Clean Slate"

There's something seductive about the "clean slate" mindset. Monday morning, January 1st, a birthday, a new notebook—it all feels fresh and full of possibility. But when you believe that real change can only happen from a clean slate, you end up constantly abandoning the messy middle.

Growth is rarely tidy. In fact, it often looks like circling back, trying again, shifting course, getting tired, and then trying one more time. And that's okay. The path to sustainable wellness isn't linear—it's layered. Each "restart" isn't erasing the past; it's building on it.

If you stopped walking for a while, you're not learning to walk again—you're picking up where you left off, but with stronger legs.

Tracking Progress Without Getting Trapped in It

One of the biggest traps in wellness culture is the obsession with metrics: weight, inches, streaks, steps. These numbers can be helpful, sure, but they can also become shackles. When progress slows or reverses, many people interpret that as failure. But that interpretation depends entirely on what story you're telling.

Instead of only tracking outcomes, consider tracking commitments. Did you show up for your morning salt water ritual three times this week, even though you were tired? That's growth. Did you pause before snacking late at night and choose what felt good instead of what felt urgent? That's a shift in awareness.

These small, internal markers of change matter—often more than the ones you can measure. They're signs that your identity is shifting, that the habits are sticking, and that you're more rooted in intention than impulse.

What "Momentum" Really Means

Momentum doesn't always feel like speed. Sometimes, it feels like getting back up quicker than you used to. Or making a better decision sooner. It's not about flawless routines—it's about shorter recovery times.

If in the past you spiraled for a week after missing a workout, and now you reset the next day—that's momentum. If you used to give up completely after a binge and now you treat yourself with compassion instead—that's momentum. You don't need acceleration. You need direction. And that's already happening, whether you see it yet or not.

The Difference Between Rigid Discipline and Rooted Discipline

A lot of wellness programs push rigid rules: drink this, eat that, never do this, always do that. The minute you break a rule, you're "off track," and the whole thing feels fragile. But there's another kind of discipline—rooted discipline. It's not about punishing yourself into compliance. It's about creating a system that can flex with your real life.

Rooted discipline is knowing what serves you, not because someone told you, but because you've felt the difference. It's choosing the pink salt water even when you don't feel like it—not out of guilt, but because it helps you think more clearly. It's understanding that some days are about full rituals and others are about just getting your bare minimum in.

This kind of discipline lasts. It bends. It adapts. And it doesn't fall apart when life gets messy.

A Different Kind of Reset

When people say "I need a reset," what they often mean is: "I need to feel like myself again." That's a powerful instinct. But instead of going to extremes—cutting out everything, restarting from zero, downloading another tracker—consider a gentler reset.

A reset can be:

- Taking one slow walk without music just to listen to your thoughts
- Revisiting your favorite wellness ritual and doing it fully, without distractions
- Drinking water with minerals before anything else in the morning
- Cleaning one drawer in your kitchen so making a good choice feels easier
- Turning off screens for 30 minutes before bed to reconnect with your own rhythms

You don't need to punish your way back to wellness. You just need to reconnect with what already works for you.

Proof That You're Not Who You Used to Be

Want evidence that you've evolved, even if it doesn't always feel like it? Look at how you talk to yourself now versus a year ago. Look at the kind of meals you crave more often. Look at how your body signals to you—and how you're starting to listen. That's not nothing. That's growth.

Old patterns may still whisper. But you don't follow them on autopilot anymore. That pause—that question mark before acting—that is the mark of change.

Even when you're tired, even when you don't get it perfect, there's a deeper part of you that wants to return. That knows what feeling good actually feels like. That has tasted clarity and doesn't want to give it up.

And that part of you? It's leading the way. Quietly. Steadily. No dramatic overhauls. Just real, lasting evolution.

So no, you're not starting over. You've already started. You're just continuing from a different place—wiser, steadier, and more aware of what truly feels like home in your body. That's not a reset. That's a return.

APPENDICES
Bonus Section

QUICK FAQ RECAP: YOUR TOP QUESTIONS, CLEARLY ANSWERED

What's the best time to drink the pink salt water?

First thing in the morning, ideally before anything else—even coffee. Your body is in a natural detox and rehydration mode after sleep. Drinking pink salt water at this time supports digestion, encourages hydration, and gently stimulates the bowels. Waiting 15–30 minutes before breakfast or caffeine gives your system time to absorb and respond.

Can I do the ritual during intermittent fasting?

Yes. A teaspoon or less of pink salt in water doesn't spike insulin and won't typically break your fast. In fact, it may help sustain your energy levels, especially if you're prone to fatigue or headaches during fasting. Just make sure you're not overdoing the salt or pairing it with caloric add-ins like honey or juice if fasting is your goal.

How much pink salt should I actually use?

Start small. Most people feel great with ⅛ to ¼ teaspoon in a full glass of filtered water. That's enough to provide trace minerals and stimulate hydration without overwhelming your system. Adjust gradually based on your body's response—especially if you're sensitive to salt or have a low-sodium diet.

What if I hate the taste?

You're not alone. Pink salt water is an acquired taste for many. Try adding a splash of lemon or a slice of cucumber to mellow the flavor. Some find room temperature water easier to drink than cold. And if it's still tough, start with a smaller glass or lower salt dose and work your way up.

Can I use regular table salt?

Nope. Table salt is stripped of natural minerals and often includes anti-caking agents that don't do your gut or cells any favors. Look for unrefined, mineral-rich salts like Himalayan pink salt or Celtic sea salt. These options support electrolyte balance, cellular function, and detox more effectively.

What does the ritual actually do for my body?

It supports cellular hydration, wakes up digestion, and helps reset electrolyte levels after a night's sleep. Many people report clearer skin, better energy, and improved bowel regularity over time.

The real benefit, though, is consistency—it acts as a morning anchor that sets the tone for better choices throughout the day.

Is this safe during pregnancy or while breastfeeding?

Always consult your provider first. Generally speaking, if you're using a small amount of high-quality mineral salt, it's safe and even supportive for many pregnant or nursing women. Hydration and mineral balance are especially important during this phase, but always personalize based on your health history.

I'm already bloated—will this make it worse?

In most cases, no. Bloating is often caused by poor digestion, sluggish lymph flow, or dehydration. Pink salt water can help stimulate natural elimination and rebalance fluid distribution. That said, if you experience bloating *immediately* after drinking, try reducing the salt or checking for other contributing factors, like food intolerances or gut dysbiosis.

What if I have high blood pressure?

Speak with your doctor before starting. While unrefined salt in small amounts behaves differently than processed sodium, your healthcare provider will know your specific risks. Some people with hypertension actually see improvements when they replace processed salt with mineral salt and reduce packaged foods, but proceed with caution.

Do I need to do this every day for it to work?

No—but the more consistent you are, the more benefits you'll see. Think of it like brushing your teeth. One day doesn't change much. But over weeks and months, the cumulative impact of regular use builds resilience and rhythm in your body. If you skip a day, don't stress. Just pick it up again the next morning.

Can I prep it the night before?

Absolutely. If mornings are chaotic, batch prep a couple of jars and keep them in the fridge. Just give it a good shake or stir before sipping. Some people even use thermal bottles to keep their mix at a preferred temperature. Whatever makes it easier to stick with—do that.

Does this replace electrolytes after workouts?

It can be a gentle support, but it's not a full replacement for intense physical exertion. For post-workout recovery, you might need additional magnesium, potassium, or sodium depending on how much you sweat. This ritual is a daily base—not a sports drink.

What kind of water should I use?

Filtered or spring water is ideal. Tap water can contain chlorine, fluoride, and other additives that may interfere with gut health or taste. Mineral water is a great option too, but not necessary if you're already getting minerals from the salt.

Can kids or teens do this?

In moderation, yes—but use a much smaller amount of salt, and always observe how their bodies respond. For young kids, ⅛ teaspoon in a small glass is usually plenty. Don't push it if they dislike the taste. You're setting up lifelong habits, and forcing it won't help.

Will this help with skin issues like acne or dullness?

It might, indirectly. Hydration and detox support both influence skin clarity. People often report a subtle glow or fewer breakouts when this becomes part of their daily rhythm. That said, skin health is multi-factorial. Don't expect overnight miracles, but this is a great foundation.

Can I do this at night instead?

You can, especially if you have trouble winding down or struggle with nighttime leg cramps (often related to magnesium or sodium deficiency). However, the morning is when the body is primed for detox and hydration. If you're doing both, use a smaller dose at night and see how your sleep feels.

Is there a "best" brand of pink salt?

Look for brands that are raw, unrefined, and free of additives. You don't need to spend a fortune. Fine or coarse both work—just choose a texture that fits your prep style. A few trustworthy sources: Redmond Real Salt, Sherpa Pink, or any certified Himalayan salt with no additives.

How long does it take to see results?

Some feel a difference within days—more regular digestion, clearer thinking, less brain fog. For others, the shift is more subtle and accumulates over weeks. Give it at least two to three consistent weeks before judging the impact. Keep an eye on how your mornings feel and whether you're reaching for sugar or caffeine less often.

Can I still drink coffee after this?

Yes, but give your body time to absorb the salt water first. Waiting 15–30 minutes before your first cup of coffee can improve hydration and reduce jitters or digestive upset. Many people find they need less caffeine once the salt ritual becomes consistent.

What if I just forget sometimes?

You're human. Don't spiral. This isn't about perfection—it's about patterns. If you forget, reset. If you miss a week, return gently. The ritual is there to support you, not to become another thing to stress about. Keep the tools visible, make it easy, and allow space for real life.

MORNING RITUAL JOURNAL PAGES (GUIDED): FOR PERSONAL REFLECTION AND MINDSET ANCHORING

Let's be honest—mornings move fast. The to-do list is already writing itself before you've opened your eyes. But carving out just five quiet minutes for yourself? That's not a luxury. That's the foundation.

This section is built like a guided journal. Not a fluffy one. Not the kind that demands calligraphy pens and watercolor margins. This one is light, flexible, and built for real-life use—even if you're still in your robe, coffee in hand, and just trying to shake off the dreams.

Each page walks you through a short morning check-in so that your mindset aligns with the body rituals you're building. This is where you anchor—not just your goals, but your awareness.

You'll use this journal to:

- Notice how your body and mind feel without judgment
- Set a daily intention instead of rushing into autopilot
- Celebrate small wins so you don't overlook them
- Practice gratitude, curiosity, and reflection in under 5 minutes

How to use these pages

Start as soon as you've finished your salt water—while it's still fresh in your system and your brain is waking up. Or jot down your answers while the kettle's heating up or your skincare is sinking in.

You don't need to answer everything every day. Let the prompts guide you, but don't feel ruled by them. Some days, one word is enough. Some days, a paragraph spills out. Both are perfect.

Feel free to print these pages, rewrite them in your own notebook, or use them digitally on your phone or tablet. It's not about the format—it's about the moment.

Morning Ritual Journal – Day 1

HOW DO I FEEL RIGHT NOW?

(Be honest, not dramatic. One word or a few. Examples: tired, hopeful, tense, grounded.)

→ _____

LAST NIGHT'S SLEEP WAS:

- Restless or broken
- Okay but interrupted
- Pretty solid
- Deep and delicious

TODAY I WANT TO FEEL:

(Pick a word—any word—that sets your intention. Calm, productive, free, focused...)

→ _____

ONE THING I CAN DO TO SUPPORT MY BODY:

→ _____

DID I HAVE MY SALT WATER?

- Yes
- Not yet, but I will
- Nope, and I'm letting that be okay

WHAT'S ONE SIGNAL MY BODY IS SENDING ME?
→ _____

THREE THINGS I'M GRATEFUL FOR TODAY:
1. _____
2. _____
3. _____

SMALL WIN FROM YESTERDAY:
→ _____

Morning Ritual Journal – Day 2

HOW DO I FEEL IN MY BODY THIS MORNING?
→ _____

ENERGY LEVEL (1 TO 5):
- 1 – Barely standing
- 2 – Moving but slow
- 3 – Neutral zone
- 4 – Alert and awake
- 5 – Let's do this

WHAT'S MY WORD FOR TODAY?
→ _____

WHAT'S ONE LOVING THING I CAN DO FOR MYSELF TODAY?
→ _____

THE SALT RITUAL FELT:
- Soothing
- Neutral
- Refreshing
- I skipped it today

ONE THOUGHT I WANT TO RELEASE:
→ _____

SOMETHING I'M LOOKING FORWARD TO:
→ _____

Variations for real-life mornings

Running late?
Just answer:
* How do I feel?
* What's my word?
* What am I grateful for?

On the go?
Use your phone's notes app to jot down three quick answers.

Feeling zero motivation?
Pick a mantra. Write it down and repeat it while brushing your teeth. Example:
"My body is not a project. It's my home."
"I choose progress, not pressure."
"One small step counts today."

Add-on prompts (optional for variety)

You can rotate these into your week if you want more reflection:

- What did I say "no" to yesterday that helped me stay on track?
- When did I feel most connected to myself this week?
- What's one area I'm growing in—even if no one else sees it?

Why it works

Your brain wakes up before your hands do. Writing—pen to paper, or thumb to screen—creates a physical act that slows your mind and opens your attention. This journal isn't for tracking. It's for witnessing.

You're not just drinking water with salt. You're choosing to wake up with intention. To listen instead of scroll. To show up with curiosity instead of criticism. And that changes everything.

Would you like me to continue with templates for Days 3–7, or develop a printable PDF version for the entire 7-day set?

7-DAY RESET REFLECTION SHEET

	DAY 1	DAY 2	DAY 3	DAY 4	DAY 5	DAY 6	DAY 7
How did you feel when you woke up?							

	DAY 1	DAY 2	DAY 3	DAY 4	DAY 5	DAY 6	DAY 7
Did you follow your pink salt ritual?							
What was your energy level like this morning?							
How was your digestion today?							
Did you experience any cravings?							
What was one small win today?							
Did anything feel off or challenging?							
What is one word to describe your mood?							
How much water did you drink (estimate)?							
Did you eat mostly whole, unprocessed foods?							
How did you move your body today?							
What is one thing you're grateful for?							
What's one thing you'd like to improve tomorrow?							

Printed in Dunstable, United Kingdom